FOUR

Metaphysical

POETS

FOUR
Metaphysical
POETS

DONNE · HERBERT
VAUGHAN · CRASHAW

With An ANTHOLOGY of Their Poetry
Especially Selected
for The VINTAGE EDITION

BY

JOAN BENNETT, M.A.

UNIVERSITY LECTURER IN ENGLISH
FELLOW OF GIRTON COLLEGE, CAMBRIDGE

NEW YORK *Vintage Books*

1 9 6 0

PUBLISHED BY VINTAGE BOOKS, INC.

Reprinted by arrangement with Cambridge University Press.

FIRST VINTAGE EDITION

First published by The Syndics of The Cambridge University Press in 1934, Second Edition in 1953.

PREFACE

to the Second Edition

I HAVE revised but not substantially altered this introduction to four seventeenth-century poets. In some ways my approach to these poets may be said to belong to the nineteen-thirties. There is an underlying assumption that the reader will be familiar with and responsive to nineteenth-century romantic poetry, and that the prosaic images, the rhythms of speech and the logical complexity of metaphysical poetry may at first repel him. Today the reader is more accustomed to difficult poetry; he no longer expects tunefulness or images that delight the senses. The qualities of lucidity and logical coherence in metaphysical poetry are more likely to seem strange to him now than the rarity of evocative rhythms and sense-delighting figures. Perhaps, today, that lucidity needs to be stressed and even excused. Modern critics often encourage us to look in poetry for fragments of meaning not wholly intended by the poet nor within his control. But the metaphysical poet knew what he meant; though rhythm and imagery enhance his meaning, they do not make it ambiguous. The only ambiguity that the reader should look for is the intentional pun, anagram or emblem. If I were beginning again today, I should find myself trying to show how, nevertheless, the best in this kind are poems and not merely witty verses. The meaning is unambiguous, but more disturbing and far-reaching than the most exact prose paraphrase. It is not only conveyed to the reason but "proved on the pulses" by the poet's rhythm and diction. These poets were skilled and subtle masters of metre, and they had something to say that required the language of poetry.

But I have not rewritten this book; I have sometimes modified a statement that now seems rash, I have expanded or rewritten sentences that now seem to me misleading or obscure, I have often expanded the quotations, giving, wherever possible, the whole poem rather than a fragment. I have also added interpretations of some stanzas which I now know (through the experience of teaching) are more difficult than I then recognized. Finally I have revised the text of the poems quoted to accord with the editions cited in the bibliographical note.

JOAN BENNETT

September 1952

A Note on the date of Donne's birth.

In previous impressions of this book I have given 1573 as the date of Donne's birth. I take this opportunity of changing this on the evidence in Professor F. P. Wilson's article entitled "Notes on the Early Life of Donne" (*Review of English Studies*, 1927) where he establishes that "Donne may have been born towards the end of 1571, or between January and June 19, 1572 . . . But it is certain that the poet was born before June 19, 1572."

J. B.

November 1956

ACKNOWLEDGEMENTS

To acknowledge one's debts is not easy, not because one is insensible of them, but for two quite other reasons. When one begins to reflect, one is overwhelmed. What ideas has one, after all, which did not grow out of some conversation or some book? Every seed was planted, a few have borne fruit. But a worse perplexity follows. Is the harvest worthy of the husbandry? Who would care to own this crop?

It is best that no one should be implicated, no names mentioned. Where my creditors are printed books they will often be obvious, but my deepest debt is to a few friends who have been as candid in criticism as they have been generous in encouragement. To one of these,[1] had it been good enough, the book would have been dedicated. But for his optimism it would not have been begun; but for his untiring helpfulness it could not have been completed.

For permission to quote copyright poems I am obliged to the Oxford University Press for *The Caged Skylark, I wake and feel the fell of dark* and *Carrion Comfort* by G. M. Hopkins; to Messrs. Burns, Oates and Washbourne, Ltd, and Mr. Wilfred Meynell for an extract from *The Hound of Heaven* by Francis Thompson; to Messrs. Faber and Faber, Ltd, and the author for an extract from *Ash Wednesday* by T. S. Eliot; to Messrs. Macmillan and Co., Ltd, and the Trustees of the Hardy Estate for *Wives in the Sere* and *In Tenebris* by Thomas Hardy; and to Messrs. Macmillan and Co., Ltd, and Mrs. Yeats for *The Folly of being Comforted, That the Night Come* and *The Rose of the World,* by W. B. Yeats.

J. B.

[1] The debt I cryptically acknowledged in 1934 was to Mr. George Rylands.

CONTENTS

FOUR

Metaphysical

POETS

CHAPTER I

Introductory

> *The extent to which images are discordant depends upon the extent to which we unfold them, and that is wholly within the poet's control, for it in turn depends primarily upon the rhythm and tempo of the writing.*
>
> MIDDLETON MURRY,
> *Countries of the Mind*

> *Neither are these only similitudes, as men of narrow observation may conceive them to be, but the same footsteps of nature, treading or printing upon several subjects or matters.*
>
> FRANCIS BACON,
> *Advancement of Learning*

THE term *metaphysical*, as applied to a group of poets who wrote under the influence of John Donne, has been consecrated by use since Dryden first employed it, in his dedication to *A Discourse concerning the Original and Progress of Satire*. It is not altogether a happy term, since it gives the impression that metaphysical poetry discusses the nature of the universe, in short, that, as Dryden assures the Earl of Dorset,

"Donne perplexes the minds of the fair sex with nice speculations of philosophy, when he should engage their hearts and entertain them with the softnesses of love." But Donne and the poets most influenced by him were not speculating about the nature of things as, for instance, Milton does in *Paradise Lost* or Pope in *The Essay on Man* or Tennyson in *In Memoriam* (for there is a similar motive in these three poems, despite all differences of temperament and of treatment). When Donne writes

> At the round earths imagin'd corners, blow
> Your trumpets, Angells, and arise, arise
> From death, you numberlesse infinities
> Of soules, . . .[1]

or even

> And new Philosophy calls all in doubt,
> The Element of fire is quite put out;
> The Sun is lost, and th'Earth, and no mans wit
> Can well direct him where to looke for it[2]

he is not defining the doctrine of the church about immortality or describing the new cosmology, he is expressing a state of mind by referring to a background of ideas. He is no more a philosophical poet because he makes use of ideas than Shelley is a descriptive poet because he makes use of things seen:

> The brightness
> Of her divinest presence trembles through
> Her limbs, as underneath a cloud of dew
> Embodied in the windless heaven of June
> Amid the splendour-wingéd stars, the moon
> Burns inextinguishably beautiful.

[1] *Holy Sonnet* VII.
[2] *An Anatomie of the World, The first Anniversary*, ll. 205 ff.

> And from her lips as from a hyacinth full
> Of honey-dew, a liquid murmur drops
> Killing the sense with passion.[3]

Shelley is not describing stars, moon, hyacinths or dew-drops; he is using them to express his sensation about Emily. Donne is not discussing whether the world is round or flat, nor the validity of the "new philosophy"; he is using these exciting speculations to express and define his emotion. In the sonnet it concerns death, judgment and eternity; in the poem it is summed up in the subtitle:

> By occasion of the untimely death of Mistress Eliza-beth Drury, the frailty and decay of this whole World is represented.

Nevertheless, Shelley used his method because he was acutely aware of sense-impressions, and Donne his, because he was acutely aware of the current of ideas. The word "metaphysical" refers to style, rather than subject-matter; but style reflects an attitude to experience. Experience to the metaphysical poets was, as it were, grist to an intellectual mill. They looked for a connection between their emotion and mental concepts. All poetical imagery arises from a perceived likeness between different things; it may be as simple as

> One ask'd me where the Roses grew?
> I bade him not goe seek;
> But forthwith bade my *Julia* shew
> A bud in either cheek.[4]

where the relation is merely a similarity in colour, touch and perhaps scent, or it may be as complex as this:

3 *Epipsychidion.*
4 Herrick.

> She lived in storm and strife,
> Her soul had such desire
> For what proud death may bring
> That it could not endure
> The common good of life,
> But lived as 'twere a king
> That packed his marriage day
> With banneret and pennon,
> Trumpet and kettledrum,
> And the outrageous cannon,
> To bundle time away
> That the night come.[5]

where a rich variety of relations is implied, relations
between human effort towards an abstract good and the
pomp, power and cruelty of kingship, things that lead
away from the common joys; and again relations between
death and the consummation of a marriage. The peculiarity of the metaphysical poets is not that they relate,
but that the relations they perceive are more often logical
than sensuous or emotional, and that they constantly connect the abstract with the concrete, the remote with the
near, and the sublime with the commonplace.

Metaphysical poetry usually comprises an analysis as
well as a correlation of emotions. A poet like Herrick,
conscientious as an artist, but, as a man, apparently free
from disturbing self-awareness, was unaffected by
Donne's influence. He sang of his religion with untrou-
bled simplicity:

> When the Temper me pursu'th
> With the sins of all my youth,
> And halfe damns me with untruth;
>   Sweet Spirit comfort me!
>
> When the flames and hellish cries
> Fright mine eares, and fright mine eyes,

[5] W. B. Yeats, *That the Night Come.*

> And all terrors me surprise;
>   Sweet Spirit comfort me!
>
> When the Judgment is reveal'd
> And that open'd which was seal'd,
> When to Thee I have appeal'd;
>   Sweet Spirit comfort me! [6]

The simplicity of rhythm and diction reflect Herrick's ease of mind. Donne's *Hymn to God the Father*, in contrast, with its meditative rhythm and its punning conclusion, communicates the self-mistrust of the more intellectual poet.

> Wilt thou forgive that sinne where I begunne,   *orig. sin. w/ Adam*
>   Which was my sin, though it were done before?
> Wilt thou forgive that sinne; through which I runne,   *his own sin*
>   And do run still: though still I do deplore?
>   When thou hast done, thou hast not done,   *Donne   donne*
>   For, I have more.
>
> Wilt thou forgive that sinne which I have wonne   *Inf. sin. to others*
>   Others to sinne? and, made my sinne their doore?
> Wilt thou forgive that sinne which I did shunne
>   A yeare, or two: but wallowed in, a score?
>   When thou hast done, thou hast not done,
>   For I have more.   *gr'test of sins — to doubt.*
>
> I have a sinne of feare, that when I have spunne   *exacting promise from god*
>   My last thred, I shall perish on the shore;
>   But sweare by thy selfe, that at my death thy sonne
>   Shall shine as he shines now, and heretofore;
>   And, having done that, Thou haste done,   *you god*
>   I fear no more.

The poets who wrote successfully in the metaphysical style were all of them self-conscious and analytic, though they vary greatly in the range and depth of their thinking and in the subtlety of their self-knowledge. Donne, for

[6] *His Letanie, to the Holy Spirit.*

instance, links up a wider range of ideas and explores a
more complex attitude of mind in "Batter my heart" than
Herbert does in *Affliction*, while Herbert's *Affliction* is
more subtle and self-aware than Vaughan's *Distraction*;
but all three are analyses of emotion. They have in common sufficient detachment from an experience, at first in-
tensely felt, to be intellectually aware of its intricacy.

Because of this analytic habit, the metaphysical poets
preferred to use words which call the mind into play,
rather than those that appeal to the senses or evoke an
emotional response through memory. Commonly the re-
verberations, or overtones, of words in poetry depend very
largely on the memory of sense-impressions they call up,
or else on the memory of emotions that the same word has
evoked in other contexts.

> No nightingale did ever chaunt
> More welcome notes to weary bands
> Of travellers in some shady haunt,
> Among Arabian sands:
>
> A voice so thrilling ne'er was heard
> In spring-time from the cuckoo-bird,
> Breaking the silence of the seas
> Among the farthest Hebrides.[7]

Unthinkingly the reader responds: the nightingale, Ara-
bian sands, spring-time and the cuckoo-bird, silent seas,
the farthest Hebrides; such words quicken emotions
which lie dormant. They awaken both sense-memories
and memories of a literary heritage. The metaphysical
poets usually neglect this accumulated treasure. If they
evoke memories, they are of "large draughts of intellectual day" imbibed from science rather than from poetry.

[7] Wordsworth, *The Solitary Reaper*.

imagery { intellectual - scientific - mechanical - geographical -

Let Maps to other, worlds on worlds have showne
Let us possesse one world, each hath one, and is one.[8]

or,

Of what supreme almightie power
Is thy great arm, which spans the east and west,
And tacks the centre to the sphere! [9]

or,

they are the hubs of love

(Though Loves whole World on us doth wheel.)[1]

We recognize that the words in such lines as these have
more than their normal prose meaning; they reverberate
as surely as do the "Arabia," the "Hebrides" and the
"cuckoo" of Wordsworth, but their stimulus is applied,
not directly to the senses or the emotions, but to something more akin to the faculty that apprehends a mathe-
matical problem.

The whole Creation shakes off night
And for thy shadow looks, the light;

writes <u>Vaughan</u> in *The Dawning,* <u>an intellectual conceit,</u>
<u>and one that sums up the metaphysical approach to ex-</u>
<u>perience.</u> It would not be wide of the mark to describe
metaphysical poetry as poetry written by men for whom
the light of day is God's shadow. The description would
apply to some secular metaphysical poems as well as to
religious; it underlies Donne's

But since my soule, whose child love is,
Takes limmes of flesh, and else could nothing doe,
More subtile then the parent is,
Love must not be, but take a body too, . . .[2]

---

[8] Donne, *The good-morrow.*
[9] Herbert, *Prayer.*
[1] Marvell, *The Definition of Love.*
[2] Donne, *Aire and Angels.*

as clearly as it underlies Herbert's description of dead bodies as

> The shells of fledge souls left behinde, . . .

An <u>intellectual bias affects</u> not only the choice of words and images, but the <u>form of their poems and their rhythmical effects</u>. Here are two poets writing in the same age and on the same theme; the first is from Nashe's play *Summer's Last Will and Testament*:

> Beauty is but a flower
> Which wrinkles will devour:
> Brightness falls from the air,
> Queens have died young and fair;
> Dust hath closed Helen's eye:
> I am sick, I must die
>   Lord have mercy upon us!
>
> Strength stoops unto the grave:
> Worms feed on Hector brave;
> Swords may not fight with fate;
> Earth still holds ope her gate;
> Come! Come! the bells do cry.
> I am sick, I must die
>   Lord have mercy upon us!

The second is Donne's sixth *Holy Sonnet*:

> This is my playes <u>last</u> scene, here heavens appoint
> My pilgrimages <u>last</u> mile; and my race
> Idly, yet quickly runne, hath this <u>last</u> pace,
> My spans <u>last</u> inch, my minutes latest point,
> And gluttonous death, will instantly unjoynt
> My body, and soule, and I shall sleepe a space,
> But my'ever-waking part shall see that face,
> Whose feare already shakes my every joynt:
> Then, as my soule, to'heaven her first seate, takes flight,
> And earth-born body, in the earth shall dwell,
> So, fall my sinnes, that all may have their right,

To where they'are bred, and would presse me, to hell.
Impute me righteous, thus purg'd of evill,
For thus I leave the world, the flesh, the devill.

Donne's pattern is the pattern of thought, of a mind
moving from the contemplation of a fact to deduction
from a fact and thence to a conclusion. The framework
of the poem is logical. Nashe's pattern is a symmetrical
design without development. Just as different is the function of rhythm in the two poems. Nashe excites emotion
by the "dying fall" of his music:

> Come! Come! the bells do cry.
> I am sick, I must die
>   Lord have mercy upon us!

Donne appeals through the ear to the intellect. The repeated "lasts" of the first four lines are the hammer
strokes of finality; in the third line the contrast between
narrow vowels and disyllables in the first half, and open
vowelled monosyllables in the second half:

> Idly, yet quickly runne, hath this last pace,

expresses the contrasted feeling. The required sense of
climax is furthered in line seven by the elision, arresting
ear and tongue so that the mind may dwell on the terrific
fact:

> But my'ever-waking part *shall see that face,*

the same close co-operation exists between meaning and
sound in

> And earth-born body, in the earth shall dwell,

with its heavy succession of monosyllables and the emphasis thrown on the verb, and in line twelve contempt
for sins is expressed in the narrow monosyllables:

> To *where* they'are *bred,* and would *presse* me, to *hell.*

Such is the part played by the ear in good metaphysical
poetry. And the imagery is similarly arresting. Instead
of touching the old springs of sorrow it sets the mind to
work anew. It is his own horror of death that Donne is
concerned with. "Gluttonous" death, waiting to "unjoint"
soul and body, like a hungry animal watching for prey:

> Queens have died young and fair;
> Dust hath closed Helen's eye:
>
> .   .   .   .   .
>
> Worms feed on Hector brave;

Nashe enriches his poem with the emotions with which
these names are stored. We feel the pity of the general
fate. But Donne is contemplating himself in the moment
of agony; it is his own peculiar sense of death that we
share, and to do so we must follow the movement of his
mind.

In metaphysical poetry emotions are shaped and expressed by logical reasoning, and both sound and picture
are subservient to this end. Words consecrated to poetry
are avoided *because* such words have accumulated emotion. The very reasons that prompt other poets to use
these words, persuade Donne and his disciples to neglect
them. Like Wordsworth they prefer words in everyday
use; but their practice goes even further than his theory.
Wordsworth proposed to use "the natural language of
impassioned feeling." [3] But the metaphysical poets use the
natural language of men when they are soberly engaged
in commerce or in scientific speculation, so that the words
themselves, apart from their meaning in the context, have
no repercussions. They cut themselves off from one of the
common means of poetry and thus become entirely de-

---

[3] The quotation is from Coleridge's *Biographia Literaria*, Ch.
xvii; but it summarizes quite justly the gist of what Wordsworth
says about poetic diction in his preface to the second edition of
Lyrical Ballads.

pendent on a successful fusion between thought and feeling; they seldom employ easy or emotionally exciting rhythms (though these are more frequent in Vaughan and Crashaw than in Donne and Herbert). Often the rhythm is as intricate as the thought and only reveals itself when the emphasis has been carefully distributed accordingly to the sense; its function is that of a stimulant, not a narcotic, to the intellect. Elizabethan rhythms were usually suggested by a classical heritage, or by the requirements of music. The rhythms of Donne and his followers are dictated by the meaning.

These peculiarities of attitude and of style have a specific value. It is not only that, as Dr. Johnson said, "to write on their plan it was at least necessary to read and think," it is perhaps even more important that it was necessary to connect, and that the same difficult achievement is required of the reader. Successful reading of metaphysical poetry necessitates at least a temporary conquest of the tendency to divorce feeling from intelligence, to be moved only at the cost of being unable to judge, and to judge well only when the sympathies are not engaged. The incompatibility of detachment and participation, or amusement and pity, is constantly impoverishing our experiences. To some extent all good literature militates against this. Any poet must separate himself from his experience if his poem is to be more than a personal outcry, and to read any good poetry exercises both judgment and sensibility. But the metaphysical poets call upon the powers of connecting in a peculiar degree; they, more than most, answer to Mr. Eliot's description of a poet as one who is "constantly amalgamating disparate experiences," who "is always forming new wholes" out of matter so diverse as "reading Spinoza, falling in love and smelling the dinner cooking." [4]

[4] *Homage to John Dryden.* Hogarth Press, 1924.

The search for the intellectual equivalents of emotion
enforces connection and it also ensures detachment. To be
handled by the intellect an experience must be held at
arm's length.

> But O alas, so long, so farre
>   Our bodies why doe wee forbeare?
> They are ours, though they are not wee, Wee are
>   The intelligences, they the spheare.
> We owe them thankes, because they thus,
>   Did us, to us, at first convay,
> Yeelded their forces, sense, to us,
>   Nor are drosse to us, but allay.[5]

Contrast the private anguish of Keats' posthumous
lines:

> You say you love; but then your hand
>   No soft squeeze for squeeze returneth,
> It is like a statue's, dead,—
>   While mine to passion burneth—
>   O love me truly![6]

Donne transmutes the personal experience of the lover
into an affirmation about the nature of man. Without
forfeiting the power to express emotion, the metaphysical
style distances the merely personal; it is not true of the
protagonist alone, but of all mankind that body and spirit
are interdependent. The two intellectual conceits point to
this conclusion.

While to its admirers the metaphysical style seems to
have peculiar merits, its detractors have naturally laid
emphasis on its peculiar faults. It has been attacked
mainly for two reasons. First, it is objected, such a style
soon degenerates into the pursuit of logical ingenuity for

[5] *The Extasie.*
[6] *Stanzas*, stanza IV.

its own sake. This is certainly the fate that overtakes it when the poet has little to say. But it is at least no worse than the pursuit of sensation for its own sake. If Donne is more ingenious than effective in *The Flea*, it may be answered that Shelley is more sensational than effective in much of *The Revolt of Islam*, and that of the two *The Flea* is the more entertaining. The second objection is that the metaphysical style is needlessly obscure. It is a more ambiguous charge, because the word obscure has such diverse meanings. It is sometimes meant that the intellectual imagery fails to communicate the poet's emotion. It is impossible to generalize as to how far, in such cases, the reader or the poet is to blame. There may actually be a cleavage between the poet's image and his original impulse; on the other hand the reader may have been unwilling or unable to make the necessary intellectual effort. The mere novelty of the problem, to those accustomed to other kinds of poetry, is an obstacle. In Wordsworth's phrase: "the poet must create the taste by which he is to be judged." The metaphysical poets demand a continual breakdown of mental habits—experiences which have been kept apart in the mind are suddenly yoked together. This often occasions what seems like obscurity in a poem, but is really only an obstruction in the reader's mind. A different cause of obscurity is the fact that some images, which were clear to the poet's contemporaries, now need elucidation. Recondite imagery is a common cause of difficulty in poetry; but a difference should be made between the almost impassable obstacle of private symbolism, such as Blake uses in his Prophetic Books, or even imagery derived from individual literary pursuits, such as Mr. Eliot uses in *The Waste Land* and, to a lesser degree, in *Ash Wednesday*; and the imagery of a poet like Donne, which demands only an acquaintance

with widespread contemporary ideas.[7] Apart from un-
wonted connections and recondite imagery, poetry may be
obscure through compression. Both Donne and Herbert
offend in this, but their very careful punctuation usually
makes the sense unambiguous. No one would contend
that they are easily read; but then few suppose that easy
accessibility is essential, or even common in good poetry.
A variety of difficulties are admissible, provided they
serve a purpose and that to overcome them affords, not
only the pleasure of a victory, but the more lasting delight of a new experience.

[7] For example, in the stanza quoted from *The Extasie*, "Wee
are The intelligences, they the spheare," depends upon the doctrine of the old astronomy which taught that the heavenly bodies
revolved round the earth in concentric spheres, each governed by
an Intelligence.

CHAPTER II

John Donne

1571–1631

> *The greatest difference between the poet and the ordinary person is found, as has often been pointed out, in the range, delicacy, and freedom of the connections he is able to make between different elements of his experience.*
>
> I. A. RICHARDS,
> *Principles of Literary Criticism*

By the time Donne began to write, the Petrarchan fashion had had its day. He was by no means the first to feel restive about it; Sir John Davies had written his *Gulling Sonnets,* others, and Shakespeare among them, had challenged and reversed the conventional pose of self-depreciation and adulation of the mistress. There was, for the moment, little more to be said about love in those terms. But there was still much to be said about love. Donne experienced that "human bondage" in most of its forms and he extended the range of lyrical expression to give tongue to what he suffered and enjoyed. The precise relation of his poetry to his biography is insoluble and not very important; what matters is that he knew enough to portray and analyse a wider

range of emotion than any other English poet except
Shakespeare. His *Songs and Sonets* and the *Elegies* may
be dramatic or they may be subjective, more probably
they are a mixture of the two, for experience and detachment are equally essential to a poet. Donne had enough
experience to realize love's many moods, from the most
brutally cynical to the most idealistic, and enough dramatic power to escape from the limits of anecdote into the
expanses of poetry. That he scorned, hated, lusted after,
loved, worshipped, there can be little doubt for anyone
who has read his poetry; and his biography confirms it.
To conjecture that particular poems belong to particular
episodes is a fascinating pursuit, but it has been too much
indulged in. It has led to few certainties and cannot in
any case do much to increase appreciation of the poetry.
To enjoy that, it is only necessary to be prepared for a
strange assortment of moods, to enter into each without
reserve, and one thing further. Donne's reader must
share, in some degree, his own capacity for associating
widely diverse themes and feelings. He travelled from
one type of experience to another, but carried with him
into the new a vivid memory of what the old had felt
like. When, for instance, after his wife's death he sought
a church as the object of his devotion, the traditional
image of the Bride of Christ fused itself in his mind with
memories of secular love. Beseeching God to reveal the
true Church he wrote:

> Betray kind husband thy spouse to our sights,
> And let myne amorous soule court thy mild Dove,
> Who is most trew, and pleasing to thee, then
> When she'is embrac'd and open to most men.[1]

The paradox was vividly realized in these terms by one
who had formerly described a man committed

---

[1] *Holy Sonnet* XVIII.

> To paths in love so dark, so dangerous:
> And those so ambush'd round with household spies,
> And over all, thy husbands towring eyes
> That flam'd with oylie sweat of jealousie.[2]

Other poets of his time emphasized the sharp divorce between their secular and sacred verses. They represented themselves as rejecting and despising their youth; but Donne recognized the unity of his experience. In *The good-morrow* he told his beloved

> If ever any beauty I did see,
> Which I desir'd, and got, t'was but a dreame of thee.

and later he declared

> Here the admyring her my mind did whett
> To seeke thee God; so streames do shew their head;[3]

and was not afraid to look back before the time when he devoted himself to Anne More, to earlier days when he could "love both faire and browne."

> As humorous is my contritione
> As my prophane Love, and as soone forgott:
> As ridlingly distemper'd, cold and hott,
> As praying, as mute; as infinite, as none.[4]

The same sense of connection enabled him to pass from the trivial to the sublime, or from jest to earnest, with an abruptness often disconcerting to readers of Milton and Wordsworth. He may begin with the magnificence of

> At the round earths imagin'd corners, blow
> Your trumpets, Angells, and arise, arise
> From death, you numberlesse infinities
> Of soules, and to your scattered bodies goe,[5]

[2] *Elegie* XII, ll. 41 ff.
[3] *Holy Sonnet* XVII.
[4] *Ibid.* XIX.
[5] *Ibid.* VII.

and continue by cataloguing a motley assortment of human ills:

> All whome warre, dearth, age, agues, tyrannies,
> Despaire, law, chance, hath slaine. . . .

It is an essential character of his mind that he recognizes trivial mundane affairs as part of the same experience as death and the dread of eternity. The tendency to segregate the sublime from the commonplace is a form of romantic idealization, more characteristic of the eighteenth and nineteenth than of the sixteenth and seventeenth centuries.

After the flood of conventional sonnet sequences in the Petrarchan fashion, poets felt the need of realism. When realism is sought as an escape from idealization, it often leads to cynicism. One affectation is replaced by its opposite. Some of Donne's poems, like his prose *Paradoxes and Problems* (which were described by John Donne the younger as "the entertainments of the author's youth"), are the products of this reaction. Their characteristics are intellectual exuberance and a spirit of contradiction. Both prose and verse writings in this mood are exercises in moral paradox, which compensate for cold affectation by bright wit and ingenious logic.

> That Women are Inconstant, I with any man confess, but that Inconstancy is a bad quality, I against any man will maintain: For everything as it is one better than another, so it is fuller of *change;* The *Heavens* themselves continually turn, the *Stars* move, the *Moon* changeth; *Fire* whirleth, *Aire* flyeth, *Water* ebbs and flowes, the face of the *Earth* altereth her looks, *time* staies not; the Colour that is most light, will take most dyes: so in Men, they that have the most reason are the most alterable in their designes, and the darkest

or most ignorant, do seldomest change; therefore Women changing more than Men, have also most *Reason.*[6]

The prose style is Euphuistic; characterized by balanced clauses and an accumulation of analogies. Donne has his tongue in his cheek; none the less his observation about the constancy of fools and the vacillations of the wise carries conviction. He is a shrewd observer and even his lightest writings are apt to contain these flashes of insight. The *Paradoxes* are a series of challenges thrown out to the morally conventional; poems in the same temper and using logic in a similar way are *The Indifferent, Confined Love, Womans constancy, The Flea* and others. In a sense they are as artificial as many an Elizabethan sonnet sequence; but at least Donne is adopting his own pose and not another's. Moreover, it is a pose which involves facing facts, if only some facts, perhaps those of which the poet was as yet aware, such as that

> Chang'd loves are but chang'd sorts of meat,
> And when hee hath the Kernell eate,
> Who doth not fling away the shell?[7]

Presently either the pose of cynicism gave place to genuine bitterness as the outcome of experience, or an increased mastery of his craft enabled Donne to express himself more convincingly. Some of the *Elegies* (I, II, IV and XII for instance) and such poems as *Loves Alchymie,* and *The Apparition,* have a convincing brutality not felt in the mocking tones of "Goe, and catche a falling starre" or "I can love both faire and browne." Jingling tunes and specious arguments are the expression and probably the outcome of lightheartedness. When he wrote like that

[6] *Paradoxes and Problems,* No. 1.
[7] *Communitie.*

Donne was impudent and unperturbed. In *The Apparition,* on the contrary, there is every sign of controlled
passion; he governs every inflection so as to convey the
cold rage of thwarted lust:

> When by thy scorne, O murdresse, I am dead,
> And that thou thinkst thee free
> From all solicitation from mee,
> Then shall my ghost come to thy bed,
> And thee, fain'd vestall, in worse armes shall see;
> Then thy sicke taper will begin to winke,
> And he, whose thou art then, being tyr'd before,
> Will, if thou stirre, or pinch to wake him, thinke
>   Thou call'st for more,
> And in false sleepe will from thee shrinke,
> And then poore Aspen wretch, neglected thou
> Bath'd in a cold quicksilver sweat wilt lye
>   A veryer ghost then I;
> What I will say, I will not tell thee now,
> Lest that preserve thee'; and since my love is spent,
> I'had rather thou shouldst painfully repent,
> Then by my threatnings rest still innocent.

The interplay of sound and meaning is masterly; the
smooth, lingering sibilants of "solicitation" surrounded by
hard monosyllables—scorne, ghost, dead, bed—matching
the contrast between what she expects and what he intends; the narrow vowels, like dagger thrusts—sicke,
pinch, winke, thinke, shrinke—and the snarling rhymes
at the end—spent, repent, innocent. Control of the sound
pattern is no less potent in producing the total effect than
is the vividness of the picture presented to the mind's eye,
the "sicke taper," the "cold quicksilver sweat," or than is
the brutal conception of the situation. There are qualities
in this poem and in the corresponding elegies which were
new to English lyrical poetry, though not to the drama.
The facts with which they deal are ugly; but they are

faced and handled with unsparing realism. The poetry does not mitigate or disguise, it enforces the crudity of the situations it portrays.

> Fond woman, which would'st have thy husband die,
> And yet complain'st of his great jealousie;
> If swolne with poyson, hee lay in'his last bed,
> His body with a sere-barke covered,
> Drawing his breath, as thick and short, as can
> The nimblest crocheting Musitian,
> Ready with loathsome vomiting to spue
> His Soule out of one hell, into a new,
>
> .   .   .   .   .
>
> Thou would'st not weepe, but jolly,'and frolicke bee,
> As a slave, which to morrow should be free;
> Yet weep'st thou, when thou seest him hungerly
> Swallow his owne death, hearts-bane jealousie.[8]

A robust delight in dialectic is the most constant feature of Donne's poetry as of his prose. His intellectual ingenuity kept pace with his emotional development, but in the lighter poems there was often little else than logical dexterity, whereas in these elegies and poems it is subservient to another kind of excitement. Passion is conveyed in images as vivid as they are violent and in the skilful management of rhythm and tempo.

It is reasonable to conjecture, from the evidence of Donne's life and correspondence, that the poems just referred to were written before he met Anne More, who was to be his wife. But they may well have been written in the same years as another set of poems conceived in quite a different temper. These are the poems that record the poignant delight of mutual love-making, without reference to outside interference, and with no hint of inadequacy in the beloved. Typical poems in this mood are

[8] *Elegie* 1, *Jealosie.*

The Sunne Rising, The Dreame, The Breake of day.
This last is the only one of Donne's poems that is put into
the mouth of a woman and it is especially interesting for
that reason. If he could imagine himself into the woman's
part, he could no doubt also imagine himself into other
situations which had no counterpart in real life. There is
no need then to suppose that every poem had its corresponding anecdote; if *The Breake of Day* is the fruit of
dramatic invention, so, probably, are many other poems,
however realistic they may be.

The Sunne Rising is remarkable for its variety of tone,
from the gay impertinence of its opening:

> Busie old foole, unruly Sunne,
> Why dost thou thus,
> Through windowes, and through curtaines call on us?
> Must to thy motions lovers seasons run?
> Sawcy pedantique wretch, goe chide
> Late schoole boyes and sowre prentices,
> Goe tell Court-huntsmen, that the King will ride,
> Call countrey ants to harvest offices;

to the full notes of satisfied love:

> Love, all alike, no season knowes, nor clyme,
> Nor houres, dayes, moneths, which are the rags of time.

and

> She'is all States, and all Princes, I,
> Nothing else is.

The poem is a successful fusion of wit and passion. *The
Dreame*, on the other hand, is written in one key. The
enjoyment of the act of love is the theme of both; the difference is that the first, through wit and raillery, takes
cognizance of the outside world, while the second nar-
rows the attention to its one object. To read the two side

by side is to get a measure of Donne's variety of treatment; he rescued English love poetry from the monotony which was threatening to engulf it at the end of the sixteenth century.

Donne could handle sensual love in all its aspects, from the bitterness of desire thwarted, to the fleeting paradise of desire fulfilled. But he was to do more than this. There are a number of poems which celebrate that rarer love in which the senses are but vehicles and mating is a "marriage of true minds." There is still no certain means of judging to whom any given poem was addressed; but we know that his relation to Anne More was of this character. Thirteen years after his marriage to her he could write: "We had not one another at so cheap a rate as that we should ever be weary of one another." The sentence strikes the same note of security as distinguishes his most mature love poetry. The need for watchful jealousy passes when the fickle senses are no longer the foundation upon which love is built. To Donne this experience was like awakening from a nightmare: he cries

> And now good morrow to our waking soules,
> Which watch not one another out of feare,[1]

or he asserts that, after their death, he and his mistress will be thought of as

> You, to whom love was peace, that now is rage.[2]

This welcome to serenity is the counterpart of his former distrust, both of his own and of his mistress's constancy. His ardent and adventurous temperament craved a point of rest, first from the love of women and later from the love of God. The triumphant close of *The Anniversarie* is the assertion of a satisfied need:

[1] *The good-morrow.*
[2] *The Canonization.*

Who is so safe as wee? where none can doe
Treason to us, except one of us two.
    True and false feares let us refraine,
Let us love nobly, and live, and adde againe
Yeares and yeares unto yeares, till we attaine
To write threescore: this is the second of our raigne.

In this phase of experience Donne does not surprise us
by wit into the acceptance of a paradox; he progresses
from thought to thought with a measured and weighty
music:

Dull sublunary lovers love
    (Whose soule is sense) cannot admit
Absence, because it doth remove
    Those things which elemented it.

But we by a love, so much refin'd
    That ourselves know not what it is,
Inter-assured of the mind,
    Care lesse, eyes, lips, and hands to misse.[3]

A new serenity is reflected in the texture of the verse.
There is no intellectual jugglery as in the earlier poems,
but a series of reasoned comparisons. Donne looks now for
intellectual figures analogous to an emotion which is itself
both felt and thought. *Aire and Angels* may not have
been addressed to his wife; but, by its intellectual music,
it belongs to the same period as the *Valedictions* and it
handles the same theme, the relation between body and
soul in sexual love:

Twice or thrice had I loved thee,
    Before I knew thy face or name;
So in a voice, so in a shapelesse flame,
Angells affect us oft, and worship'd bee;

[3] *A Valediction: forbidding mourning.*

Still when, to where thou wert, I came,
Some lovely glorious nothing I did see.
　　But since my soule, whose child love is,
Takes limmes of flesh, and else could nothing doe,
　　More subtile then the parent is,
Love must not be, but take a body too,
　　And therefore what thou wert, and who,
　　　　I bid Love aske, and now
That it assume thy body, I allow,
And fixe it selfe in thy lip, eye, and brow.

Whilst thus to ballast love, I thought,
And so more steddily to have gone,
With wares which would sinke admiration,
I saw, I had loves pinnace overfraught,
　　Ev'ry thy haire for love to worke upon
Is much too much, some fitter must be sought;
　　For, nor in nothing, nor in things
Extreme, and scatt'ring bright, can love inhere;
　　Then as an Angell, face, and rings
Of aire, not pure as it, yet pure doth weare,
　　So thy love may be my loves spheare;
　　　　Just such disparitie
As is twixt Aire and Angells puritie,
'Twixt womens love, and mens will ever bee.

That is a difficult poem for the modern reader to understand; some have supposed that the closing couplet, affirming as it does that woman's love is necessarily less pure than man's, is an expression of cynicism. But it is Donne's habit to strike his keynote in the first lines of a poem; if the reader's final impression is in a different key, he should suspect himself of misinterpreting. So when Donne begins:

Twice or thrice had I loved thee,
　　Before I knew thy face or name;

we should expect a poem in the mood of *The good-morrow* which contains the similar statement:

> If ever any beauty I did see,
> Which I desir'd, and got, t'was but a dreame of thee.

His cynical poems begin with such lines as

> I can love both faire and browne,

or, more bitterly:

> When by thy scorne, O murdresse, I am dead,

In the first stanza of *Aire and Angels* Donne is saying much what he says in *The Extasie*, man is a body as well as a soul; love is the child of the soul, but the soul itself can do nothing in this world without the body:

> More subtile then the parent is,
> Love must not be, but take a body too,

Therefore the god of love is asked to find out who or what is the "lovely glorious nothing." And the god shows Donne his fair mistress, such as Elizabethan sonneteers described, with her "lip, eye, and brow."

But, in the second stanza, Donne rejects the lady's physical charms as the object of his love. He uses a metaphor in which his love is a ship and he is looking for wares to ballast it. His admiration (wonder) is the keel; but the lady's physical charms instead of making the keel ride steadily through the water will be likely to sink the ship. He decides that love can no more reside in every bright hair of his mistress's head than in "some lovely glorious nothing." He then introduces the figure that gives the poem its title. Angels, in medieval angelology, manifested themselves to men by assuming "wings and face of aire" because air was the purest of the four elements. Yet air, since it is a terrestrial element is less pure

than the angel in its supernatural state. The lady's love
for him, Donne is saying, can embody his love for her as
the air embodies the angel. It will be a sphere in which
his love will rule as intelligences rule the heavenly
spheres. In the "great chain of being," reaching down
from God to the lowest of His creatures, woman is next
below man, just as the human pair are above animals,
vegetable life and minerals, that is why the woman's love
is as much less ethereal than the man's as air is less ethereal than angelic substance. The man's love as described
in the first stanza was aspiration after the ideal, he has
now found that ideal manifested in the woman's love for
him. The brilliant ingenuity displayed in such a poem as
The Flea has developed into a logical subtlety capable of
expressing complex emotion. Donne could by now con-
ceive and express a love which, though it belongs as
much to the body as to the mind, is strong in absence
and even independent of external beauty. In *Elegie* v he
leaves his picture with his mistress before going on a
journey. When he returns the picture may be no likeness:

> If rivall fooles taxe thee to'have lov'd a man,
> So foule, and course, as, Oh, I may seeme than,
> This shall say what I was: and thou shalt say,
> Doe his hurts reach mee? doth my worth decay?
> Or doe they reach his judging minde, that hee
> Should now love lesse, what hee did love to see?
> That which in him was faire and delicate,
> Was but the milke, which in loves childish state
> Did nurse it: who now is growne strong enough
> To feed on that, which to disused tasts seemes tough.

The relation between mind and body, the security of a
love in which that relation has been fully established,
and the unity of lovers are the themes of Donne's maturity. They are themes which concern all lovers and

they refute the implication of Dryden's famous criticism.
Dryden's picture of Donne who "perplexes the minds of
the fair sex with nice speculations of philosophy"[4] is
profoundly misleading. He may use such speculations as
an instrument; but his own inquiries in his poetry are
about love itself:

> Me thinkes I lyed all winter, when I swore,
> My love was infinite, if spring make'it more.[5]

or

> Thou canst not every day give me thy heart,
> If thou canst give it, then thou never gavest it.[6]

"The metaphysics" occur in his poetry as a vehicle, but
never as the thing conveyed.

Before and during his married years Donne enjoyed
the friendship of women and these friendships gave rise
to a number of poems concerning a relation between man
and woman in which, for some reason, physical union is
denied. In *The Undertaking* he claims such a relation as
an ideal, desirable in itself, but beyond the reach of most
men:

> If, as I have, you also doe
>   Virtue'attir'd in woman see,
> And dare love that, and say so too,
>   And forget the Hee and Shee;
>
> .   .   .   .   .
>
> Then you have done a braver thing
>   Than all the *Worthies* did;
> And a braver thence will spring,
>   Which is, to keep that hid.

---

[4] Dedication to *A Discourse concerning the Original and
Progress of Satire.*
[5] *Loves growth.*
[6] *Lovers infinitenesse.*

More often he is disturbed by the <u>sense of incomplete-</u>
<u>ness</u>. His intellect rebels against the restraint that has
been imposed. He claims to have obeyed the rules, but
not to have accepted them:

> Comming and going, wee
> Perchance might kisse, but not between those meales;
> Our hands ne'r toucht the seales,
> Which nature, <u>injur'd by late law</u>, sets free:[7]

The parenthesis in the last quoted line sounds the note
of rebellion. In *Twicknam garden* he complains more
bitterly against the impossibility of possessing his beloved; the last couplet is his grudging acceptance of the
facts:

> O perverse sexe, where none is true but shee,
> Who's therefore true, because her truth kills mee.

In *The Blossome* he proposes to wean his heart from an
unyielding lover and to give it

> . . . to another friend, whom wee shall finde
> As glad to have my body, as my minde.

Unlike Herbert, Vaughan and Crashaw, Donne never,
even in his religious poetry, belittled physical love; no
poet has paid more consistent homage to a complete
human relationship.

After his wife's death he sought in religion for the
sense of security and completeness that she had at one
time given him. Religion had always been of great intellectual interest for him. Born and bred a Roman Catholic he accepted the Church of England (outside of
which all preferment in church or state was barred to
him), but not without a struggle. In *Satyre* III, written

[7] *The Relique.*

between 1593 and 1595, he considers the relative claims
of nonconformity, Anglicanism and Roman Catholicism.
Already religion and the search for the true church are
of grave importance to him:

> . . . though truth and falsehood bee
> Neare twins, yet truth a little elder is;
> Be busie to seeke her, beleeve me this,
> Hee's not of none, nor worst, that seekes the best.
> To adore, or scorne an image, or protest,
> May all be bad; doubt wisely; in strange way
> To stand inquiring right, is not to stray;
> To sleepe, or runne wrong, is. On a huge hill,
> Cragged, and steep, Truth stands, and hee that will
> Reach her, about must, and about must goe;
> And what the hills suddennes resists, winne so;
>
> Yet strive so, that before age, deaths twilight,
> Thy Soule rest, for none can worke in that night.

In the *Holy Sonnets* the desire for intellectual rest is
interwoven with a need for the emotional serenity he had
tasted in marriage. He cries out to God in the accents of
love:

> Take mee to you, imprison mee, for I
> Except you'enthrall mee, never shall be free,
> Nor ever chast, except you ravish mee.[8]

He expresses his love for God in terms of that of a lover
for his mistress, or, as here, a woman for her lover, he
trusts and mistrusts God's pity as the lover vacillates between the secure sense of being loved and the recurrent
fear that love may yet be withdrawn:

> What if this present were the worlds last night?
> Marke in my heart, O Soule, where thou dost dwell,

---

[8] *Holy Sonnet* xiv.

The picture of Christ crucified, and tell
Whether that countenance can thee affright,

.   .   .   .

No, no; but as in my idolatrie
I said to all my profane mistresses,
Beauty, of pitty, foulnesse onely is
A signe of rigour: so I say to thee,
To wicked spirits are horrid shapes assign'd,
This beauteous forme assures a pitious minde.[9]

In the religious poetry Donne explores his feelings towards God just as, in the secular poetry, he explored his
feelings towards the beloved. He defines the intricate
balance of his attitude with similar subtlety, although, as
already in the mature love poetry, delight in paradox has
given place to the perception of interrelations. In the
religious poetry, as in the secular, profound emotion
works upon Donne's intellect not as a narcotic but as a
stimulant.

The *Litany,* composed in 1609, must have been among
the earliest of Donne's religious poems. Sir Edmund
Gosse dismissed it as a "cold work of the intellect," but
its measured tone is the result, not of coldness, but of the
marriage of thought and feeling. It has an intricate slow
music which suggests thinking aloud:

From being anxious, or secure,
Dead clods of sadnesse, or light squibs of mirth,
From thinking, that great courts immure
All, or no happinesse, or that this earth
Is only for our prison fram'd,
Or that thou art covetous
To them whom thou lovest, or that they are maim'd
From reaching this worlds sweet, who seek thee thus,
With all their might, Good Lord deliver us.

[9] *Ibid.* XIII.

Balance and serenity is reflected in the quietness of the
rhythm, the struggle through which it has been achieved
is expressed in the close-packed thought. The mind of
the reader is continually checked, not by the surprise of
paradox but by the sense of balance and sufficiency upon
which the mind pauses as thought after thought receives
its complement:

> From needing danger, to bee good,
> From owing thee yesterdaies teares to day,
> From trusting so much to thy blood,
> That in that hope, wee wound our soule away,
> From bribing thee with Almes, to excuse
> Some sinne more burdenous,
> From light affecting, in religion, newes,
> From thinking us all soule, neglecting thus
> Our mutual duties, Lord deliver us.

This low-toned music, compelling the reader to adopt the
deliberate pace of meditation without losing the rhythm
of impassioned earnestness, is a rare achievement in
poetry. Mr. T. S. Eliot in *Ash Wednesday*, a poem whose
mood of tranquillity after conflict is not unlike that of
Donne's *Litany*, achieves by the movement of the verse
a similar effect, as of emotion held in check and regulated
by thought. Both poems are, of course, based on liturgical
patterns:

> Consequently I rejoice, having to construct something
> Upon which to rejoice
>
> And pray to God to have mercy upon us
> And I pray that I may forget
> These matters that with myself I too much discuss
> Too much explain
> Because I do not hope to turn again
> Let these words answer

For what is done, not to be done again
May the judgment not be too heavy upon us

Because these wings are no longer wings to fly
But merely vans to beat the air
The air which is now thoroughly small and dry
Smaller and dryer than the will
Teach us to care and not to care
Teach us to sit still.

This rapid survey has attempted no more than an indication of the diversity of Donne's poetry. Because of
the alternation of his moods and the range of his experience, and because his poems have inevitably been printed
without reference to a chronological order, it seemed
necessary to indicate the variety of tone and intention
comprised in them, as a preliminary to a study of his
poetic method.

CHAPTER III

Donne's Technical Originality

> *Sensibility alters from generation to generation, whether we will or no, expression is only altered by a man of genius.*
>
> T. S. ELIOT

ONNE's technique was in many ways a new thing in English poetry and his most important innovations, although they found imitators among his immediate successors, afterwards remained in abeyance for two centuries. The practice of Milton and his many imitators, of the eighteenth-century poets, or of the nineteenth century, with the exception of Gerard Manley Hopkins, show small trace of Donne's influence. Milton's Eve is

> Like a wood nymph light
> Oread or Dryad, or of Delia's train.

Burns sings of one of his lady-loves:

> I see her in the dewy flowers
> I see her sweet and fair:
> I hear her in the tunefu' birds,
> I hear her charm the air:

Shelley tells of

> A Lady the wonder of her kind,
> Whose form was upborne by a lovely mind
> Which, dilating, had moulded her mien and motion
> Like a sea-flower unfolded beneath the ocean.

However much they differ, these poets use what seems like the same language compared with Donne, who likens his mistress to a hemisphere or one arm of a pair of compasses, speaks of her hair as a viceroy and her tears as coins or maps.

Donne had a different conception of the function of imagery from that of these other poets. The purpose of an image in his poetry is to define the emotional experience by an intellectual parallel. It is as essential to follow his reasoning when reading, as it is to respond to Keats' sense perception of dethroned Saturn when

> Upon the sodden ground
> His old right hand lay nerveless, listless, dead,
> Unsceptred; and his realmless eyes were closed.

Keats' sensuous impression is identified with the thing he wants to express; Donne, on the other hand, identifies his intellectual analogy with his emotion. A great part of the value of his poetry, to those who enjoy him, lies in the demand he thus makes on the imagination in the sense in which Coleridge defines it: "judgment ever awake and steady self-possession with enthusiasm and feeling profound or vehement." [1]

Donne's reader must be capable, not only of feeling and thinking at the same time; but even of simultaneously sharing an emotion and enjoying a joke. He must move as easily as Donne himself from the mood of the first stanza of *The Sunne Rising* to that of the last; or

---

[1] *Biographia Literaria*, c. XIV.

from the sardonic temper of the opening lines of *The Relique* to the poignancy of what follows:

> When my grave is broke up againe
> Some second ghest to entertaine,
> (For graves have learn'd that woman-head
> To be to more then one a Bed)
>   And he that digs it, spies
> A bracelet of bright haire about the bone,
>   Will he not let'us alone,
> And thinke that there a loving couple lies,
> Who thought that this device might be some way
> To make their soules, at the last busie day,
> Meet at this grave, and make a little stay?

The parenthesis is not irrelevant, it points the contrast between the common run of women and that "not impossible she" whom he describes in the last lines:

>   But now alas,
> All measure, and all language, I should passe,
> Should I tell what a miracle shee was.

His images are drawn from his own interests, so that he is always illustrating one facet of his experience by another. Everything that played an important part in his life or left its mark upon his mind occurs in the poetry, not as subject-matter, but as imagery. His subject-matter was, as has been seen, confined almost entirely to various aspects of love and of religion; but his imagery reveals the width of his intellectual explorations.

He was widely read in most of the subjects that excited cultivated minds in his day: astronomy, chemistry, geography, physiology, law, and theology, and he drew upon all these indifferently for illustration. Dr. Johnson mitigates his strictures on the metaphysical poets by allowing that "if their conceits were far-fetched they were often worth the carriage," but, in Donne's case at any rate, they were not far-fetched, they were a part of his everyday life. Today, there can be nothing to surprise us in a lively interest in astronomy; Copernicus, Kepler and Galileo were for Donne's contemporaries what Einstein is for us. The facts they were discovering about the universe affected thought as radically. The scepticism of the modern astronomers about law and logic in stellar movements, was paralleled in the seventeenth century by scepticism about the central position of the earth. In each case the new theory revolutionizes the conception of man's importance in relation to the whole. Donne might well assume that his readers would respond to imagery drawn from so vital an issue. He expressed no opinion as to the facts. Nowhere, either in verse or prose, does he argue about Ptolemaic or Copernican systems; he used either indifferently or the conflict between the two, for the expression of something else. In *An Anatomie of the World, The first Anniversary*, where, by occasion of the anniversary of the death of Elizabeth Drury, Donne mourns the decay of morals, he uses the new philosophy as an illustration. It is the symptom, perhaps partly the cause, of the breaking up of the medieval world-order:

> And new Philosophy calls all in doubt,
> The Element of fire is quite put out;
> The Sun is lost, and th'Earth, and no mans wit
> Can well direct him where to looke for it.
> And freely men confesse that this world's spent,
> When in the Planets, and the Firmament
> They seeke so many new; they see that this
> Is crumbled out againe to his Atomies.
> 'Tis all in peeces, all cohaerence gone;
> All just supply, and all Relation:
> Prince, Subject, Father, Sonne, are things forgot,

> For every man alone thinkes he hath got
> To be a Phoenix, and that then can bee
> None of that kinde, of which he is, but hee.[2]

But more often, in his poetry, <u>Donne draws his images from the old astronomy.</u> In *Good Friday, 1613, Riding Westward* he <u>used the scholastic doctrine of the spheres, each governed by an intelligence or angel;</u>[3] and the Ptolemaic doctrine of cycles and epicycles:

> Let mans Soule be a Spheare, and then, in this,
> The intelligence that moves, devotion is,
> And as the other Spheares, by being growne
> Subject to forraigne motions, lose their owne,
> And being by others hurried every day,
> Scarce in a yeare their naturall forme obey:
> Pleasure or businesse, so, our Soules admit
> For their first mover, and are whirld by it.

Again in *A Valediction: forbidding mourning* he uses an old-fashioned Ptolemaic doctrine:

> Moving of th'earth brings harmes and feares,
>   Men reckon what it did and meant,
> But trepidation of the spheares,
>   Though greater farre, is innocent.

whilst in a verse letter to Lady Bedford he adopts the new Copernican teaching about a moving earth and stationary sun. The poetry tells us nothing about Donne's intellectual attitude to astronomy, except that he was aware both of obsolete and of recent theories.

He drew as freely and, from a scientific point of view, as indiscriminately, on contemporary chemical ideas, mak-

---

[2] *An Anatomie of the World, The first Anniversary*, ll. 205 ff.
[3] The same doctrine of intelligences governing spheres is used in *The Extasie* and in *Aire and Angels*. It owed its origin to St. Thomas Aquinas, though it was not rejected by Kepler. (See article on Astrology, *Enc. Brit.*)

ing use of the latest scientific theory, or of current super-
stition, as each served his purpose. His various references
to alchemy are typical. Sometimes he accepts it as valid,
sometimes he assumes it is all imposture. In a verse letter
To the Countesse of Huntingdon the doctrine of tran-
substantiation and the alchemical theory of the trans-
mutation of metals together express the notion that the
spirit of the dead has entered into the living. He is
speaking of the Countess's sister recently dead:

> She guilded us: But you are gold, and Shee;
>> Us she inform'd, but transubstantiates you;
> Soft dispositions which ductile bee,
>> Elixarlike, she makes not cleane, but new.

In *An Anatomie of the World*, to describe Elizabeth
Drury as immune from the stain of the fall, he speaks of
her as

> . . . She that could drive
> The poysonous tincture, and the staine of *Eve*,
> Out of her thoughts, and deeds; and purifie
> All, by a true religious Alchymie;[4]

In *Loves Alchymie*, on the other hand;

> Oh, 'tis imposture all:
> And as no chymique yet th'Elixar got,
>> But glorifies his pregnant pot,
>> If by the way to him befall
> Some odoriferous thing, or medicinall,
>> So, lovers dreame a rich and long delight,
>> But get a winter-seeming summers night.

Increasing knowledge of the world's surface was caus-
ing as much excitement as increasing knowledge of the
Cosmos in Donne's lifetime so that, as was to be expected,
he frequently made use of geographical images. Examples

4 *The first Anniversary.*

will be found in *The good-morrow; A Valediction: Of
the Booke* (last stanza); *Hymn to God my God in my
Sicknesse;* and in *An Anatomie of the World, The first
Anniversary.* As far as the evidence of the poetry goes,
Donne had no more and no less knowledge of contemporary geographical theories than an intelligent, well-
read man today normally acquires of astronomy or psychology; but, because all subjects which invite the play
of the mind were his delight, all such subjects occur to
him in his mood of poetic creation.

Donne's physiological imagery has caused more com-
ment than that drawn from other sciences, partly because
of its frequent occurrence, both in prose and verse, and
partly because it has aroused disgust in certain readers.
He has been accused of morbidness, a charge supported
by his elaborate preparations for his own funeral and his
masochistic dwelling in his last sermon on "the wormes
that shall feed and feed sweetly upon us." In the first
place it must be remembered that physiology at the beginning of the seventeenth century was as unmapped and
exciting a territory as were astronomy and geography, or
as psychology is today. No one who has scanned the pages
of Burton will doubt its fertility. Mrs. Simpson tells us
in her *Study of the Prose Works of John Donne* that,
while he was studying law, between 1590 and 1601,
Donne also mastered "the grounds and use of physique."
His contemporary, Lord Herbert of Cherbury, thought
such study an essential part of the education of a gentleman. Inevitably, living when he did, and with his
"immoderate, hydroptique thirst for human learning,"
Donne was interested in medicine and inevitably, therefore, he made use of medical ideas to define his emotional
experiences. Moreover, Donne's intellectual interest in
medicine was probably re-enforced by the sorrows of his
seventeen years of married life, during which several of

his children died, he himself was repeatedly ill, and finally his wife died, worn out with poverty and sickness. It is no wonder that images from disease and dissolution haunt his later prose and verse. His desire for God is a dropsy:

> But though I have found thee, and thou my thirst
> has fed,
> A holy thirsty dropsy melts mee yett.[5]

The coming and going of his religious fervour is an ague:

> So my devout fitts come and go away
> Like a fantastique Ague: save that here
> Those are my best dayes, when I shake with feare.[6]

Two of his best known love poems have as their central symbol

> A bracelet of bright haire about the bone,

which will keep his skeleton from dissolution, or will be worshipped for a relic after his death.

But the prevalence of the facts of death and disease, both in his verse and in his prose, is not only due to an intellectual interest in physiology. It is the counterpart of his delight in the life of the senses. He is as medieval in his insistence on the grave and the narrow margin that divides the skeleton from the living face, as he is in his scholastic delight in the processes of reasoning. His is an attitude to the body that belongs to a time when death lurked round every corner, the gift of plague, famine or violence. Realistic and familiar treatment of the physical facts of death is not peculiar to Donne; it is the mark of his age, it stamps the pages of Webster, of Burton, of Jeremy Taylor no less than Donne's own. The men of the

[5] *Holy Sonnet* XVII.
[6] *Holy Sonnet* XIX.

Middle Ages and of the Renaissance knew that life is but
a moment; they valued it the more highly and especially
those aspects of it which vanish most certainly. The more
the life of the senses is valued, the more terrible and insistent the fact of its transience becomes and also the
physical incidence of death. One may thrust these down
into the unconscious, but this was never Donne's way nor
the way of his contemporaries. With him as with them a
full rich physical life brought into prominence the fact of
mortality, in a way which is perhaps less morbid than its
opposite, the "hush! hush!" attitude to disease and death.

The nature of Donne's imagery accounts for some of
the strangeness felt by a modern reader who encounters
his poetry for the first time. The nemesis of being very
actual in one's own generation is often that one appears
strange to those that succeed. But the difficulty of merely
deciphering Donne's meaning has been much exag-
gerated. The force of his image is nearly always apparent
from the context, even when the doctrine of which it
forms a part is forgotten.[7] The real difficulty is not to
discern what might be described as the "prose meaning,"
but to allow an image, which must first be seized intellectually, subsequently to affect one's whole sensibility:

> Shee'is dead; And all which die
>   To their first Elements resolve;
> And wee were mutuall Elements to us,
>   And made of one another.
> My body then doth hers involve,
> And those things whereof I consist, hereby
> In me abundant grow, and burdenous,
>   And nourish not, but smother.[8]

[7] At the worst this kind of difficulty, due to the reader's igno-
rance of contemporary ideas, can often be removed by a reference
to Professor Grierson's notes in the Clarendon Press edition.
[8] *The Dissolution.*

To arrive at the meaning we need only know of the theory that death is the breaking up of a compound into its elements; a theory stated by the verse itself. But to arrive at the meaning is not the same as to experience the poem. When Hardy writes:

> Wintertime nighs;
> But my bereavement-pain
> It cannot bring again:
> Twice no one dies.
>
> Flower petals flee;
> But, since it once hath been,
> No more that severing scene
> Can harrow me.
>
> Birds faint in dread:
> I shall not lose old strength
> In the lone frost's black length:
> Strength long since fled! [9]

a train of emotionally relevant associations troop into the mind. Winter, the falling flowers, birds in bleak weather, frost and the blackened earth all echo the sense of bereavement. The images touch the same keys as the loss they represent, whereas Donne's analogy needs to be thought through to its consequences before we feel with him.

When Yeats in his early poetry (in his later poems he preferred a more austere and, in a sense, a more metaphysical style) required an hyperbole he made use of the reader's remembered emotions:

> Who dreamed that beauty passes like a dream?
> For these red lips with all their mournful pride,
> Mournful that no new wonder may betide,

[9] *In Tenebris*, first three stanzas.

Troy passed away in one high funeral gleam,
And Usna's children died.

.   .   .   .

Bow down, archangels, in your dim abode:
Before you were, or any hearts to beat,
Weary and kind one lingered by His seat;
He made the world to be a grassy road
Before her wandering feet.[1]

All the sorrow and glory that adheres to the legends of
Greece or of Ireland are used by the poet to evoke the
state of mind he requires. Donne frequently employs the
device of hyperbole; but it operates in a different way.

O wrangling schooles, that search what fire
    Shall burne this world, had none the wit
Unto this knowledge to aspire,
    That this her feaver might be it?[2]

Unless the image awakens some of the excitement about
ideas which impelled the scholastic Fathers, Donne's
reader will remain unmoved. It is not difficult to understand the stanza, it may be difficult to respond to it with
the feeling the poem requires. Donne's images must be
followed logically; point by point they fit the emotion
illustrated. In *Loves growth,* for instance, in image after
image Donne probes into a universal experience; descant-
ing on the rebirth of love in the spring-time; asserting
finally:

And yet no greater, but more eminent,
    Love by the spring is growne;
    As, in the firmament,
Starres by the Sunne are not inlarg'd but showne.
Gentle love deeds, as blossomes on a bough,

---

[1] *The Rose of the World.*
[2] *A Feaver.*

From loves awakened root do bud out now.
If, as in water stir'd more circles bee
Produc'd by one, love such additions take,
Those like so many spheares, but one heaven make,
For, they are all concentrique unto thee.
And though each spring doe adde to love new heate,
As princes doe in times of action get
New taxes, and remit them not in peace,
No winter shall abate the springs encrease.

The words which in other poetry would bring with them
an aura of association and require no further reflection,
such words as *starres, sunne, blossomes, spring, root,* and
bud, operate differently in Donne's poem. We need to
follow intellectually the relation of each to the subject.
If we are to enjoy Donne, such activity must be in itself
a delight. The words which strike the keynote of the
poem are *circles, spheares, concentrique;* these are the
symbols of that infinity in love which underlies the
human ebb and flow. The circle occurs again and again
in Donne's verse and in his prose as the symbol of infinity. Insensibility to such intellectual symbolism has
caused not only Dr. Johnson but even so modern a critic
as Miss Sackville-West to cite the compass image, in *A
Valediction: forbidding mourning,* as an example of metaphysical ineptitude.[3]

We expect from poetry something which is often called
"verbal magic," whereby the single word, in its context,
assumes a richer significance than that which ordinarily
belongs to it. This is owing largely to the sequence of
sounds; but also largely, in most poetry, to the associated
memories of emotion and sensation that the word brings
with it. Donne's words bring with them the memory of

[3] In her *Andrew Marvell,* Hogarth Press (The Poets on the
Poets).

abstract ideas. The magical lines in his poetry are those
which evoke such conceptions as those of space, time,
nothingness, eternity:

> Let Maps to other, worlds on worlds have shown.[4]

> Love, all alike, no season knowes, nor clyme,
> Nor houres, dayes, moneths, which are the rags of time.[5]

> He ruin'd mee, and I am re-begot
> Of absence, darknesse, death; things which are not.[6]

> All changing unchang'd Antient of dayes.[7]

The lovely vowel music of this last line is certainly a
part of its magic. It is rare for Donne to make this kind
of use of his sound-pattern. His conception of rhythm was
as original as his diction and imagery, and many critics,
even down to our own times, have echoed Ben Jonson's
judgment that "Donne for not keeping of accent deserves
hanging."

He forsook the simple tunes of the Elizabethans which
dictate the accent of joy or sorrow:

> Love for such a cherry lip
> Would be glad to pawn his arrows;
> Venus here to take a sip
> Would sell her doves and team of sparrows.
> > But they shall not so;
> > Hey nonny, nonny no!
> > None but I this lip must owe,
> > Hey nonny, nonny no!

And the sad cadences of

> Weep you no more, sad fountains;
> What need you flow so fast?

[4] *The good-morrow.*
[5] *The Sunne Rising.*
[6] *A nocturnall upon S. Lucies day.*
[7] *Holy Sonnets. La Corona.*

> Look how the snowy mountains
> Heaven's sun doth gently waste.
>> But my sun's heavenly eyes
>> View not your weeping,
>> That now lies sleeping
>> Softly, now softly lies
>>> Sleeping.

To tunes like these we are accustomed in poetry, we respond to the emotion even before the meaning of the words has been fully registered; Bridges communicates breathless delight with the lilt of

> When June is come, then all the day
> I'll sit with my love in the scented hay:
> And watch the sun-shot palaces high,
> That the white clouds build in the breezy sky.

Or Shelley strikes the note of a funeral bell with

> Death feeds on his mute voice and laughs at our despair.

But Donne rejoices and grieves in intricate patterns that work through the mind; he announces his pinnacle of joy in the measured tones of thought:

> True and false feares let us refraine,
> Let us love nobly, and live, and adde againe
> Yeares and yeares unto yeares, till we attaine
> To write threescore: this is the second of our raigne;[8]

and his elegiac music forces us to dwell on the meaning of the words and the linking of thought with thought:

> 'Tis the yeares midnight, and it is the dayes,
> *Lucies,* who scarce seaven houres herself unmaskes,
>> The Sunne is spent, and now his flasks
>> Send forth light squibs, no constant rayes;
>>> The worlds whole sap is sunke:

[8] *The Anniversarie.*

> The generall balme th'hydroptique earth hath drunk,
> Whither, as to the beds-feet, life is shrunke,
> Dead and enterr'd; yet all these seeme to laugh,
> Compar'd with mee, who am their Epitaph.[9]

The monosyllables fall like hammerstrokes; then the
sound dies away in the short line

> The worlds whole sap is sunke:

and increases again in volume in the lines that follow
with the full tones of "the generall balme th'hydroptique
earth" and the numbing thuds of sound: "sunke,"
"drunk," "shrunke," "dead"; lightened with an effect of
sardonic bitterness in the soft rhymes "laugh: epitaph";
every twist and turn in the sound pattern is a preparative
for the despair expressed in the central conceit of the
poem:

> I, by loves limbecke, am the grave
> Of all, that's nothing.

Donne deliberately deprived himself of the hypnotic
power with which a regularly recurring beat plays upon
the nerves. He needed rhythm for another purpose; his
rhythms arrest and goad the reader, never quite fulfilling
his expectations but forcing him to pause here and to
rush on there, governing pace and emphasis so as to
bring out the full force of the meaning. Traditional

---

[9] *A nocturnall upon S. Lucies day, Being the shortest day.* Mr.
Doniphan Louthan argues persuasively that the occasion of this
poem was the marriage of Lucy Harrington to Edward Russell,
third Earl of Bedford, Dec. 12th, 1594; the poem would be a
lament for the loss of the beloved, but not by her physical death.
See *The Poetry of John Donne. An Explication.* Bookman Associates, New York. The phrase "as to the beds-feet" has been found
obscure. It was believed that the departing soul retreated, at the
moment of death, to the foot of the bed, cf. Bunyan, *The Life
and Death of Mr. Badman,* ". . . and look, there stands the devil
at my beds feet to receive my soul when I die."

imagery and traditional rhythms are associated with traditional attitudes; but Donne wanted to express the complexity of his own moods, crude or subtle, harmonious or
discordant. He had to find a more personal imagery and
a more flexible rhythm. He made demands on his reader
that no lyric poet had hitherto made. It is easy to miss his
sound patterns through careless reading, because so much
depends on the right distribution of pause and emphasis.
His principal innovation was to make the cadences of
speech the staple of his rhythm; contemporary dramatists
had done this in blank verse, but no one had so far attempted it in lyrical poetry. It is this which makes the
opening lines of his poems often so arresting:

> Now thou hast lov'd me one whole day,
> To morrow when thou leav'st, what wilt thou say? [1]

or

> He is starke mad, who ever sayes,
> That he hath beene in love an houre, [2]

or

> If yet I have not all thy love,
> Deare, I shall never have it all. [3]

Set in such different emotional keys, these opening lines
are alike in their successful rendering of the accent of
speech. It is speech of a peculiar kind, not the rhetorical
speech of Dryden's verse, not the nimble give and take
of dialogue, such as Pope gives in his *Epistle to Arbuth-
not* nor yet the simple speech rhythms of Hardy at his
best. It is a dramatic rhythm which gives the illusion of
talk in a state of excitement:

[1] *Woman's constancy.*
[2] *The broken heart.*
[3] *Lovers infinitenesse.*

> Oh doe not die, for I shall hate
>   All women so, when thou art gone,[4] . . .

Nothing could be closer to the spoken word or more apparently inevitable. With the further elaboration of the thought that follows, the rhythm becomes more complicated:

> O wrangling schooles, that search what fire
>   Shall burne this world, had none the wit
> Unto this knowledge to aspire,
>   That this her feaver might be it?
>
> And yet shee cannot wast by this,
>   Nor long beare this torturing wrong,
> For much corruption needfull is
>   To fuell such a feaver long.

The inverted feet in the second stanza emphasize the words denoting pain; both the sound pattern and the sense demand slower reading:

> Nor lóng | beáre this | tórturing | wróng.

Constantly it will be found that reading aloud, by someone sensitive to the dramatic value of words, discovers a deliberate intention in Donne's irregularities:

> *Love,* any devill else but you,
> Would for a given Soule give something too.
> At Court your fellowes every day,
> Give th'art of Riming, Huntsmanship, or Play,
> For them which were their owne before;
> Onely I have nothing which gave more,
> But am, alas, by being lowly, lower.[5]

The general inharmoniousness reflects the discordant mood, and a clear and effective sound pattern emerges when the emphasis is thrown strongly on the important

---

[4] *A Feaver.*
[5] *Loves exchange.*

words, for instance on "given" in line 2, on "I" and "gave" in line 6.

Donne's rhythm demands variety of pace. He has been called the most rapid of poets, and also the slowest. Both statements are true. A poem may begin slowly and presently hurry the reader into a rapidity that is almost breathless.

> For every houre that thou wilt spare mee now,
>> I will allow,
> Usurious God of Love, twenty to thee,
> When with my browne, my gray haires equall bee;

So far a measured and dignified bargaining:

> Till then, Love, let my body raigne, and let
> Mee travell, sojourne, snatch, plot, have, forget,
> Resume my last yeares relict: thinke that yet
>> We'had never met.[6]

The pace increases through the successive monosyllables "let"—"let," "snatch, plot, have, forget" down to the staccato of the last short line. Equally hurried is the opening verse of *The Canonization*:

> For Godsake hold your tongue, and let me love,
>> Or chide my palsie, or my gout,
> My five gray haires, or ruin'd fortune flout,
>> With wealth your state, your minde with Arts im-
>>> prove,
>> Take you a course, get you a place,
>> Observe his honour, or his grace,
> Or the Kings reall, or his stamped face
>> Contemplate, what you will, approve,
>> So you will let me love.

And Donne continues to race through the catalogue of advice to would-be carpers, finally slowing down to the pomp of the last lines:

[6] *Loves Usury.*

And by these hymnes, all shall approve
Us *Canoniz'd* for Love:

And thus invoke us; You whom reverend love
Made one anothers hermitage;
You, to whom love was peace, that now is rage;
Who did the whole worlds soule contract, and drove
Into the glasses of your eyes
(So made such mirrors, and such spies,
That they did all to you epitomize,)
Countries, Townes, Courts: Beg from above
A patterne of your love!

Certain poems demand a slow and measured reading
throughout, for instance *The Dreame, A Valediction:
Of Weeping,* and *The Anniversarie,* with the magnificent pomp of its opening stanza:

All Kings, and all their favorites,
All glory of honors, beauties, wits,
The Sun it selfe, which makes times, as they passe,
Is elder by a yeare, now, then it was
When thou and I first one another saw:
All other things, to their destruction draw,
Only our love hath no decay;
This, no to morrow hath, nor yesterday,
Running it never runs from us away,
But truly keepes his first, last, everlasting day,

through the slow intricacy of the central stanza and on to
the restrained passion of the close. If the reading is any-
where hurried, much of the poem's richness is lost. *A
nocturnall upon S. Lucies day,* already quoted, is equally
slow and needs sensitive reading aloud to produce its full
effect. That it must be read slowly is obvious; the difficulty here is to allow the pauses required by the sense,
without losing the sound pattern, when the sense runs on
from line to line. A similar difficulty is commonly experi-

enced in reading blank verse aloud, and particularly the blank verse of Donne's contemporaries, Webster or Middleton. Too marked a pause or too little can equally well mar the rhythm. The same type of difficulty occurs in reading a poet who resembles Donne in some ways, Gerard Manley Hopkins. Hopkins, like Donne, governs the emphasis with great subtlety. He uses Donne's trick of breaking up the lines suddenly, indicating a pause or intake of breath by means of an exclamatory monosyllable:

> But ah, but O thou terrible, why wouldst thou rude on
>   me
> Thy wring-world right foot rock? lay a lionlimb against
>   me? scan
> With darksome devouring eyes my bruiséd bones? and
>   fan,
> O in turns of tempest, me heaped there; me frantic to
>   avoid thee and flee? [7]

Compare Donne's use of the monosyllable "Oh":

> If rivall fooles taxe thee to'have lov'd a man,
> So foule, and course, as, Oh, I may seeme than. [8]

> I planted knowledge and life's tree in thee,
> Which Oh, shall strangers taste? [9]

> I, like an usurpt towne, to'another due,
> Labour to'admit you, but Oh, to no end, [1]

> She that, Oh, broke her faith, would soon breake thee. [2]

Hopkins is like Donne too in the interweaving and opposition between the pauses dictated by the meaning and those dictated by the pattern:

[7] Gerard Manley Hopkins, *Carrion Comfort.*
[8] *Elegie* v.
[9] *Elegie* vii.
[1] *Holy Sonnet* xiv.
[2] *A Jeat Ring Sent.*

O the mind, mind has mountains; cliffs of fall
Frightful, sheer, no-man-fathomed. Hold them cheap
May who ne'er hung there. Nor does long our small
Durance deal with that steep or deep. Here! creep,
Wretch, under a comfort serves in a whirlwind: all
Life death does end and each day dies with sleep.[3]

Donne's basic metre is the iambic five foot line. Ben
Jonson complained of his "not keeping of accent"; sometimes he shifts the stress from the second to the first
syllable of a foot, sometimes he introduces extra syllables,
indicating that they should be slurred. For instance:

I, like | an ús|urpt tówne |, to'áno|ther dúe,
Lábour | to'admít | you, bút | Óh, to | no énd,
Réason | your více|roy in mée, | me shóuld | defénd,
But ís | captív'd, | and próves | wéake or | untrúe.

Hopkins uses "sprung rhythm" which he describes as
follows: "To speak shortly, it consists in scanning by
accents or stresses alone, without any account of the number of syllables, so that a foot may be one strong syllable
or it may be many light and one strong."[4]

Both poets ring their changes on the rhythm of spoken
English, their variations reflect the emotions of an impassioned speaker. Both poets are governed by metrical laws
but both prefer a flexible system. Their patterns are
dramatic, they appear to arise out of the needs of the
moment rather than to be imposed beforehand.

None of Donne's immediate successors had his wide
range of emotional experience, none needed his wide
variety of rhythmical pattern. But his principal innovations were freely copied. The simplicity and seeming in-
evitability of phrase which is one of Herbert's most strik-

[3] No. 41, in Robert Bridges' edition, O.U.P.
[4] *The Correspondence of Gerard Manley Hopkins and Richard
Watson Dixon*, edited by Claud Colleer Abbott. Letter III.

ing characteristics owes its origin to Donne who, it is
sometimes forgotten, was as capable of simplicity as of
subtlety. The derivation of Herbert's rhythms is best seen
when Donne is remembered as the poet of such lines as

> All day, the same our postures were,
>   And wee said nothing, all the day.[5]

> What ere she meant by'it, bury it with me,[6]

> That love is weake, where feare's as strong as hee;[7]

or

> Why should we rise, because 'tis light?
> Did we lie downe, because 'twas night?[8]

The moving tones of human speech, grown metrical in
apparently inevitable response to the feeling that prompts
it, is not the least of the gifts Donne bestowed on the
poets who were influenced by him.

[5] *The Extasie.*
[6] *The Funerall.*
[7] *The Dreame.*
[8] *Breake of day.*

CHAPTER IV

George Herbert

1593–1633

❧❧

Cannot thy love
Heighten a spirit to sound out thy praise
As well as any she?
GEORGE HERBERT

ERBERT's mother, Magdalene Herbert, was the addressee of several of Donne's poems and letters. When she died he made for her a magnificent funeral oration; he must often have visited that house which he describes as "a court in the conversation of the best" and George Herbert must have been early acquainted with manuscripts of his poetry. The influence of the elder poet on the younger was strong and permanent. Herbert's imagery, like Donne's, works through the mind rather than the senses and the structure of his poems is logical. But, for various reasons, his poetry is simpler than Donne's. The range of his experience was narrower. Donne expresses hate, disgust, jealousy, lust, love, reverence, security and mistrust. He traverses every variety of mood, both as a lover and as a worshipper; and at any given moment the experiences he has already passed through are still present to him. Each poem rep-

resents a complex state of mind and a subtle adjustment
of impulses. Herbert's narrower experience not only
limits his choice of subject-matter, but simplifies the texture of his poems.

At an early age Herbert decided that the emotional
peace and satisfaction he sought was not to be found in
the love of women. He shut himself off from the whole
field of experience in which Donne's *Songs and Sonets*
found their origin. His mother was the only woman to
whom he ever addressed a poem. When he was only four
years old his father died and Magdalene Herbert was free
to give all her devotion and shaping influence to her
children. She moved with little George to Oxford, where
Edward was then studying, and remained there for four
years, with both her sons under her eye, George working
with tutors and Edward reading for his degree. After-
ward she moved with George to London and he went as
a day-boy to Westminster College. Not till 1609, the
year in which he entered the university, did his mother
marry again; so that, throughout his childhood and
adolescence, and right up to the threshold of manhood,
he had been closely and lovingly watched over by a
mother who, as we know, was no ordinary woman. Izaak
Walton speaks of her "great and harmlesse wit, her cheerful gravity and obliging behaviour," but Donne, in his
funeral sermon, draws a stronger portrait. He tells us of
her "inclination and conversation, naturally cheerful, and
merry, and loving facetiousness, and sharpnesse of
wit . . . ," and, with impassioned eloquence, he tells of
her generosity to the plague-stricken: "of which, myself,
who, at that time, had the favour to be admitted into that
family, can, and must testify this, that when the late heavy
visitation fell hotly upon this towne, when every doore
was shut up, and, lest Death should enter into the house,
every house was made a sepulchre of them that were in

it, then, then, in that time of infection, diverse persons visited with that infection, had their releefe, and releefe applicable to that very infection, from this house." And, finally, he tells us how "In the doctrine, and discipline of that Church, in which God sealed her to himselfe in Baptisme, shee brought up her children, she assisted her family, she dedicated her soule to God in her life and surrendered it to him in her death; and in that forme of Common Prayer, which is ordained by that Church, and to which she accustomed herself, with her family, twice every day, she joined with that company, which was about her death bed." We are left with the picture of a woman of quick intelligence, unusual courage, firmness of will and strong religious zeal, who coveted her son's devotion, not for herself, but for the Church. She had always intended George for the Church; soldiering was the family profession, but for this he had not the physique and he resigned himself, at first reluctantly, to an academic career which was to end in a country parsonage. For New Year's day 1610 he sent to his mother his first two poems. The theme of both was the inadequacy of earthly loves. In an accompanying letter he declared that he did not need the help of the muses "to reprove the vanity of those many love poems that are daily writ, and consecrated to Venus; nor to bewail that so few are writ that look towards God and heaven. For my own part, my meaning (dear mother) is, in these sonnets, to declare my resolution to be, that my poor abilities in poetry, shall be all and ever consecrated to God's glory." The sonnets show the influence of Donne; the first begins with a question, the second with a statement, each perfectly reproducing the accent of the spoken word:

> My God, where is that ancient heat towards thee,
> Wherewith whole showls of *Martyrs* once did burn,
>   Besides their other flames? Doth Poetry

> Wear *Venus* Livery? only serve her turn?
> Why are not *Sonnets* made of thee? and layes
>   Upon thine Altar burnt? Cannot thy love
>   Heighten a spirit to sound out thy praise
> As well as any she? Cannot thy *Dove*
> Out-strip their *Cupid* easily in flight?

The macabre jest about the flames is in the metaphysical tradition, as is the conceit with which the second sonnet closes:

> Open the bones, and you shall nothing find
>   In the best *face* but *filth*, when, Lord, in thee
>   The *beauty* lies in the *discovery*.

Herbert never wavered in his resolution to devote his poetic gifts exclusively to the service of God. In a poem called *Dulnesse,* we find him again drawing a parallel between his own theme and that of the love poet:

> The wanton lover in a curious strain
>   Can praise his fairest fair;
> And with quaint metaphors her curled hair
>   Curl o're again.
>
> Thou art my lovelinesse, my life, my light,
>   Beautie alone to me:
> Thy bloudy death and undeserv'd, makes thee
>   Pure red and white.

And the same conscious choice of the love of God as alternative to the love of women prompts *A Parodie,* in which Herbert follows the pattern of a song once thought to have been by Donne,

> Soules joy, now I am gone,
>   And you alone,
>   (Which cannot be,
> Since I must leave myselfe with thee,
>   And carry thee with me)

> Yet when unto our eyes
>   Absence denyes
>   Each others sight,
> And makes to us a constant night,
>   When others change to light
>   *O give no way to griefe,*
>   *But let beliefe*
>   *Of mutuall love,*
>   *This wonder to the vulgar prove*
>   *Our Bodyes, not wee move.*[1]

For Herbert it is God, not an earthly lover, whose absence is inconceivable:

> Souls joy, when thou art gone,
>   And I alone,
>   Which cannot be,
> Because thou dost abide with me,
>   And I depend on thee;

Herbert married Jane Danvers in 1629; he was thirty-six years old and in failing health. It was a childless though, we are told, a happy marriage. Herbert died four years later. A year after his marriage he accepted the living of Bemerton. The two events were not unconnected. Marriage was a carefully considered step in his consecration to God's service. In the prose treatise called *The Country Parson* we learn what he thought about a married priesthood:

> The Country Parson considering that virginity is a higher state then Matrimony, and that the Ministry requires the best and highest things, is rather unmarried, then marryed. But yet as the temper of his body may be, or as the temper of his Parish may be, where he may have occasion to converse with women,

[1] Sir Herbert Grierson prints this among the poems attributed to Donne (Appendix B viii, *Song*, probably by the Earl of Pembroke).

and that among suspicious men, . . . he is rather married then unmarried.

And of the choice of a wife he writes:

If he be married, the choyce of his wife was made
rather by his eare, then by his eye; his judgement, not
his affection found out a fit wife for him, whose humble, and liberall disposition he preferred before beauty,
riches, or honour.[2]

Thus circumspectly, in strong contrast to the headlong
impetuosity of John Donne, Herbert probably chose his
own wife.

But it must not be supposed that Herbert was of a
placid or equable temperament. Lord Herbert of Cherbury tells us in his autobiography that "my brother
George was not exempt from passion and choler (being
infirmities to which all our race is subject)." And Herbert, in his autobiographical poems *Affliction*, speaks of
his "fierce and sudden" youth; the poems often describe
his servitude to God as a bondage against which he vainly
rebels.

> I struck the board, and cry'd, No more.
>   I will abroad.
>   What? shall I ever sigh and pine?
> My lines and life are free; free as the rode,
>   Loose as the winde, as large as store.
>   Shall I be still in suit?
> Have I no harvest but a thorn
> To let me bloud, and not restore
> What I have lost with cordiall fruit?
>   Sure there was wine
> Before my sighs did drie it: there was corn
>   Before my tears did drown it.

[2] *A Priest to the Temple or the Country Parson his Character*
etc. Chap. IX.

> Is the yeare onely lost to me?
> Have I no bayes to crown it?
> No flowers, no garlands gay? all blasted?
> All wasted?

The Collar, which is this poem's title, is an emblem of
servitude. The poem moves through rebellion against his
Master to the sudden recognition that the freedom he is
claiming is freedom from God's love:

> But as I rav'd and grew more fierce and wilde
> At every word,
> Me thoughts I heard one calling, *Child!*
> And I reply'd, *My Lord.*

His poetry is not the record of quiet saintliness, but of
continual wrestling and continual submission; the collar
is not easily worn:

> I know the wayes of Pleasure, the sweet strains,
> The lullings and the relishes of it;
> The propositions of hot bloud and brains;
> What mirth and musick mean; what love and wit
> Have done these twentie hundred yeares, and more:
> I know the projects of unbridled store:
> My stuffe is flesh, not brasse; my senses live,
> And grumble oft, that they have more in me
> Then he that curbs them, being but one to five:
> Yet I love thee.[3]

No human love competed with the love of God for Herbert; but the fuller life of worldly intercourse and the
sweets of ambition allured him: he complains in *Affliction* (1):

> Whereas my birth and spirit rather took
> The way that takes the town;
> Thou didst betray me to a lingring book,
> And wrap me in a gown.

---

[3] *The Pearl. Matth.* 13. 45.

Charles Cotton speaks of him as

> He whose education
> Manners and parts, by high applauses blown,
> Was deeply tainted by Ambition,
> And fitted for a court, . . .[4]

which is in keeping with Herbert's confession in *Afflic-tion* (1), that:

> Thou often didst with Academick praise
> Melt and dissolve my rage.

and in *The Country Parson* he describes ambition as one of the commonest and most insidious temptations with which men of his calling can be afflicted:

> Ambition, or untimely desire of promotion to an higher state or place, under colour of accommodation or necessary provision, is a common temptation to men of any eminency. . . .

This was the temptation that Herbert resisted, though not without rebellion and remonstrance:

> Were it not better to bestow
> Some place and power on me?
> Then should thy praises with me grow,
> And share in my degree.

he urges in *Submission*,

> But when I thus dispute and grieve,
> I do resume my sight,
> And pilfring what I once did give,
> Disseize thee of thy right.

To reject God, for Herbert, would be to prefer the prizes and praises of the world to the act of loving, for God has

[4] Quoted by George Herbert Palmer in his edition of *The English Works of George Herbert*. Houghton Mifflin & Co. 3 vols., 1905; revised, 1907; reissued, 1915.

no rival in his heart. That is why he suffers so acutely
under the ebb and flow of his own zeal:

> How should I praise thee, Lord! how should my rymes
>   Gladly engrave thy love in steel,
> If what my soul doth feel sometimes,
>   My soul might ever feel! [5]

No theme occurs more frequently, or is more poignantly
expressed, than this distress at the dying away of emotion:

> Whither away delight?
> Thou cam'st but now; wilt thou so soon depart,
>   And give me up to night? [6]

His over-mastering desire is to be allowed to love God;
the need expressed in the passionate paradox with which
Affliction (1) closes. He has toyed with the thought of
seeking some other service and suddenly he turns back
to his first and only love with the despairing cry:

> Ah my deare God! though I am clean forgot,
> Let me not love thee, if I love thee not.

Herbert's poetry is the expression of an ardent temperament with a single emotional outlet.

With the exception of a few didactic poems interpret-
ing the doctrine or ritual of the Church, all his poetry is
spiritual autobiography. The devotional poet, perhaps
even more than the love poet, is exposed to the danger of
confiding in his public instead of writing poems. His problem is to build a structure that will stand alone, in-
dependently of either the reader's or the poet's private
concerns. It is here that the "Donne tradition" is salutary.
Within that tradition the structure of a poem is normally
dialectic. Herbert states his premises with precision, usually by means of an image, in the tone of a prose argu-

[5] *The Temper* (1).
[6] *The Glimpse.*

ment. The reader is never befogged; the words represent clear-cut ideas which are the medium through which the poet's emotion is conveyed as well as, often, the cause of that emotion. Herbert knows and states what he thinks, as well as what he feels, about, for example, death and immortality or the relation between God and the soul. This does not mean that his poems are arguments designed to persuade the reader. Herbert takes the reader's intellectual assent for granted. He writes for his fellow-Christian. The substance of each poem is emotional, but the emotion is rooted in thought. As the reader absorbs the poem he becomes aware of that fusion between thought and feeling which constitutes the poet's belief. Suspension of his own irrelevant incredulities is easier than it is with poetry whose intellectual structure is less self-sufficient. A comparison will make the difference clearer. Herbert in a poem called *Death* and Tennyson in stanza cxxix of *In Memoriam,* each assert a belief in immortality. Tennyson addresses the spirit of his dead friend:

> Thy voice is on the rolling air;
> > I hear thee where the waters run;
> > Thou standest in the rising sun,
> And in the setting thou art fair.

> What art thou then? I cannot guess;
> > But tho' I seem in star and flower
> > To feel thee some diffusive power,
> I do not therefore love thee less:

> My love involves the love before;
> > My love is vaster passion now;
> > Tho' mix'd with God and Nature thou,
> I seem to love thee more and more.

> Far off thou art, but ever nigh;
> > I have thee still, and I rejoice;

I prosper, circled with thy voice;
I shall not lose thee tho' I die.

A statement in the first stanza is followed in the second
by a question to which no answer is forthcoming:

What art thou then? I cannot guess;

and in the third and fourth stanzas there are further
statements again, but they are intentionally vague. The
words "I seem" dominate the stanza, the total impression
left with the reader is that Tennyson perhaps knew what
he felt, but certainly not what he thought. Herbert's
poem *Death* is based on the premise that the death of
Christ is the pledge of our resurrection; that he assumes
this is made plain in the poem by the juxtaposition of
two contrasted pictures representing the pre-Christian
and the Christian view of death:

Death, thou wast once an uncouth hideous thing,
            Nothing but bones,
        The sad effect of sadder grones:
Thy mouth was open, but thou couldst not sing.

For we consider'd thee as at some six
            Or ten yeares hence,
        After the losse of life and sense,
Flesh being turn'd to dust, and bones to sticks.

We lookt on this side of thee, shooting short;
            Where we did finde
        The shells of fledge souls left behinde,
Dry dust, which sheds no teares, but may extort.

But since our Saviours death did put some bloud
            Into thy face;
        Thou art grown fair and full of grace,
Much in request, much sought for as a good.

> For we do now behold thee gay and glad,
> As at dooms-day;
> When souls shall wear their new aray,
> And all thy bones with beautie shall be clad.

> Therefore we can go die as sleep, and trust
> Half that we have
> Unto an honest faithfull grave;
> Making our pillows either down, or dust.

The plot of the poem is clear and simple, three stanzas to describe death as it seemed before the resurrection, culminating in the lucid and lovely image of bodies that were but

> The shells of fledge souls left behinde,

which (with its suggestion of spring and birth) leads on to three stanzas describing death as it seems since the resurrection. The concrete imagery builds up two clearly contrasted pictures, each impregnated with its appropriate feeling, the horror of death the skeleton

> Thy mouth was open, but thou couldst not sing.

and the peace of death

> As at dooms-day;
> When souls shall wear their new aray,
> And all thy bones with beautie shall be clad.

A modern reader may be in closer sympathy with Tennyson's indecision, but his stanza remains unsatisfactory as poetry, because he does not say what he means, nor quite mean what he says. Herbert, like Donne, was capable of clear thought in conjunction with vehement feeling. The two kinds of activity abetted each other, so that the logical plotting of a lyric suited his genius. But he modified Donne's style in other respects. His experiences were less

complex, less varied, so that he could convey them more
simply. He used words more widely current and more
often selected his illustrations from every day life. In two
poems called *Jordan,* Herbert describes his stylistic aims,
setting them out in conscious distinction both from the
elaborateness of the Petrarchists and from the intellectual
subtlety of Donne:

> Is it no verse, except enchanted groves
> And sudden arbours shadow course-spunne lines?
> Must purling streams refresh a lovers loves?
> Must all be vail'd, while he that reades, divines,
>   Catching the sense at two removes?
>
> Shepherds are honest people; let them sing:
> Riddle who list, for me, and pull for Prime:
> I envie no mans nightingale or spring;
> Nor let them punish me with loss of rime,
>   Who plainly say, *My God, My King.*[7]

Herbert will not have pastoral affectations, neither will
he have the intellectual curiosities of Donne.

> When first my lines of heav'nly joyes made mention,
> Such was their lustre, they did so excell,
> That I sought out quaint words, and trim invention;
> My thoughts began to burnish, sprout, and swell,
> Curling with metaphors a plain intention,
> Decking the sense, as if it were to sell.
>
> Thousands of notions in my brain did runne,
> Off'ring their service, if I were not sped:
> I often blotted what I had begunne;
> This was not quick enough, and that was dead.
> Nothing could seem too rich to clothe the sunne,
> Much lesse those joyes which trample on his head.

---

[7] *Jordan* (1). F. E. Hutchinson in his invaluable edition *The
Works of George Herbert* (Clarendon Press, 1941) explains "pull
for Prime"; it refers to the card game primero in which the player
draws for a card or cards which will make him *prime.*

As flames do work and winde, when they ascend,
So I did weave my self into the sense.
But while I bustled, I might heare a friend
Whisper, *How wide is all this long pretence!*
There is in love a sweetnesse readie penn'd:
Copie out onely that, and save expense.[8]

The two poems not only describe the kind of simplicity Herbert intends, they also illustrate the simplicity
he achieves. It is the result of concrete imagery, familiar
diction and a sound pattern close to the rhythm of speech.
He chooses words that recall the affairs of every day. His
lines are "course-spunne" and his imagery of the market
place. He creates for us, in the second poem, the picture
of a bustling salesman, fidgeting about his wares, "deck-
ing the sense, as if it were to sell," until he is advised to
"save expense." This is the kind of image he always
prefers, an image which associates his experience with the
daily traffic of men of affairs or with ordinary household
business. When, in *Church-lock and key,* he wants to
describe his flagging zeal, he likens himself to a cold man
impatiently bullying an insufficient fire:

> But as cold hands are angrie with the fire,
> And mend it still;
> So I do lay the want of my desire,
> Not on my sinnes, or coldnesse, but thy will.

In *Confession* grief tortures a man as a carpenter tortures
wood or an illness the body:

> No scrue, no piercer can
> Into a piece of timber work and winde,
> As Gods afflictions into man,
> When he a torture hath design'd.
> They are too subtill for the sub'tllest hearts;
> And fall, like rheumes, upon the tendrest parts.

[8] *Jordan* (11).

He gains his effects from the short, strong, familiar words
of daily usage:

> My throat, my soul is hoarse;
> My heart is wither'd like a ground
> Which thou dost curse.
> My thoughts turn round,
> And make me giddie; Lord, I fall,
> Yet call.[9]

Herbert often invented rhyme schemes or metrical patterns to illustrate the experience conveyed in the poem.
In *Longing,* for instance, each stanza comes to rest in a
two-foot line, which reflects the moment of exhaustion
after stress:

> Look on my sorrows round!
> Mark well my furnace! O what flames,
> What heat abound!
> What griefs, what shames!
> Consider, Lord; Lord, bow thine eare,
> And heare!

The strong contrasts of crescendo and diminuendo are a
favourite device with him. This and other emblematic
uses of metre are effective for Herbert because he re-
creates regular patterns of feeling. Despite his use of
logic, his poems rarely progress (as Donne's do) to an
unforeseen conclusion. When they seem to do that (as
in *The Collar*) the surprise is reserved for the last lines.
The steps towards the resolution of an emotional problem, in Herbert's poems, are as similar to one another as
are the stanza-forms that communicate them. They advance, retreat, tread firmly, haltingly, or whatever it may
be, in regular sequences. In *Deniall* Herbert invents a
metre and rhyme scheme to reflect the broken relationship between God and the soul:

[9] *Longing.*

When my devotions could not pierce
    Thy silent eares;
Then was my heart broken, as was my verse:
    My breast was full of fears
        And disorder:

Each stanza ends with a short unrhymed line until the last, where the rhyme is completed to suggest the renewed harmonious relation with God that the poet desires.

O cheer and tune my heartlesse breast,
        Deferre no time;
That so thy favours granting my request,
        They and my minde may chime,
            And mend my ryme.[1]

Poets of more complex moods cannot deal so simply with the problem of relating sound to sense, their pattern cannot be predetermined with the same completeness. But what Herbert had to say was usually simple and the kind of device he invented was often admirable for his purpose. At times he went so far as to arrange a pattern for the eye as well as for the ear; in *The Altar* and in *Easter-wings* the subject is represented by the shape of the print upon the page.

It is a naïve device but adequate to the simple mood in which it was conceived. The effect of *Easter-wings* is less jejune than is sometimes supposed, for Herbert was sufficiently master of his instrument to make a double use of the pattern. The shape of the wings on the page may have meant more when Emblem Books were popular,[2] the diminuendo and crescendo that bring it about are expressive both of the rise and fall of the lark's song and

---

[1] *Deniall.*
[2] See the chapter on George Herbert in *English Emblem Books* by Rosemary Freeman. London, 1948.

flight (Herbert's image) and also of the fall of man and his resurrection in Christ (the subject that the image represents).

Lord, who createdst man in wealth and store,
Though foolishly he lost the same,
   Decaying more and more,
      Till he became
         Most poore:
         With thee
      O let me rise
   As larks, harmoniously,
And sing this day thy victories:
Then shall the fall further the flight in me.

My tender age in sorrow did beginne:
And still with sicknesses and shame
   Thou didst so punish sinne,
      That I became
         Most thinne.
         With thee
      Let me combine
   And feel this day thy victorie:
For, if I imp my wing on thine,
Affliction shall advance the flight in me.³

Herbert's poetry, despite his aristocratic birth and breeding and his considerable learning, leaves the impression of an unsophisticated mind. In certain ways the appeal of his verse is similar to the appeal of John Bunyan's prose. Like Bunyan, though for other reasons, he drew his language and imagery from daily affairs or from his religion. To understand him demands no culture that is not shared by all his co-religionists, and by the many more who are acquainted with the Bible and the teaching of the English church. But besides its simplicity in this sense, Herbert's poetry, like Bunyan's prose, exhibits cer-

³ *imp my wing*: to imp, in falconry, is "to engraft feathers in a damaged wing, so as to restore and improve the powers of flight" (O.E.D.) [quoted from F. E. Hutchinson, *ed. cit.*].

tain childlike qualities of mind—the playfulness of some of his metrical effects is a case in point; a trick, for instance, like that of *Trinitie Sunday* in which three three-lined stanzas with triple rhymes represent the subject:

> Lord, who hast form'd me out of mud,
>   And hast redeem'd me through thy bloud,
>   And sanctifi'd me to do good;
>
> Purge all my sinnes done heretofore:
>   For I confesse my heavie score,
>   And I will strive to sinne no more.
>
> Enrich my heart, mouth, hands in me,
>   With faith, with hope, with charitie;
>   That I may runne, rise, rest with thee.

Such devices convey a child-like quality of mind, native to Herbert perhaps, or else acquired in obedience to the injunction "except ye become as one of these little ones." Patterns akin to the acrostic appealed to Herbert, he liked word games. In the poem *Paradise* for instance, cutting off the initial letter of the rhyme word represents God pruning his tree:

> I blesse thee, Lord, because I GROW
> Among thy trees, which in a ROW
> To thee both fruit and order OW,

and so on for five stanzas. Such playful effects as these, though exceptional in Herbert's work, indicate a fundamental difference between his mind and Donne's which accounts for other modifications he made in the metaphysical style.

Herbert profited from every aspect of Donne's style, but he always adapted it to his own temperament. He simplified the inner logical pattern, following as a rule a single train of argument; he changed the metrical pattern

into something less flexible, though still studying to relate
sound to sense; he narrowed the range of diction and
imagery, while preserving their actuality. Similarly he
adapted Donne's manner of accenting the line so as to
reproduce the tone of the spoken word:

> I, like an usurp'd towne, to'another due,
> Labour to'admit you, but Oh, to no end,

writes Donne. This is the rhythm of speech, but only
such as men speak under the stress of excitement. There
is a suggestion of breathlessness, when we read the line
we pant with the effort it describes. This was seldom the
effect Herbert required, he preferred the tone of men ex-
changing news in the market place:

> Having been tenant long to a rich Lord,
> Not thriving, I resolved to be bold,[4]

It is on this level that Herbert's poems open, our attention is held, but our expectation is low pitched:

> My God, I heard this day,
> That none doth build a stately habitation
> But he that means to dwell therein.[5]

The relation between such an accent and the openings of
Donne's poems is clear; Herbert like his master avoids the
poetical, the words seem to fall into the natural prose
order and to conform without effort to the metrical
mould. But the climate of emotion is different:

> For Godsake hold your tongue, and let me love!

writes Donne, or

> What if this present were the worlds last night?

[4] *Redemption.*
[5] *Man.*

No poet can afford to start at such a pitch unless he can sustain it or increase the tension. Herbert must start in low tones if we are to get the full impact of his climax, which consists often in a subtle change of feeling or attitude. His most characteristic gift is the power of controlling the movement of feeling in his poems. The emotional pattern is managed with exquisite tact. The attitudes he handles are subtle and delicate, over emphasis or emphasis in the wrong place, over haste or too much delay, would destroy their effect; but in such matters Herbert is a master. The opening lines of his poems are usually quiet, they place the reader at the heart of the subject just as Donne does, but, unlike Donne, Herbert maintains a demeanour of calm and restraint, and this is so even when, like Donne, he opens with an exclamation or question:

> Oh that I could a sinne once see! [6]

> It cannot be. Where is that mightie joy
> Which just now took up all my heart? [7]

> Oh, what a thing is man! How farre from power,
> From setled peace and rest! [8]

The mood is collected, it is the preparation for a discussion of the theme. A similar difference is noticeable between the closing lines of Herbert's poems and those of Donne or of Hopkins. Herbert constantly achieves his effect by relaxing the tension at the end of a poem. The struggle is over and all is peace. *The Thanksgiving,* for instance, is a discussion with God, in which the poet tries to offer an equivalent for all that has been given:

[6] *Sinne* (11).
[7] *The Temper* (11).
[8] *Giddinesse.*

> If thou shalt give me wit, it shall appeare,
>   If thou hast giv'n it me, 'tis here.
> Nay, I will reade thy book, and never move
>   Till I have found therein thy love,
> Thy art of love, which I'le turn back on thee:
>   O my deare Saviour, Victorie!

and then the poet falters and the culminating point of
the poem suggests a lowering of the voice almost to a
whisper:

> Then for thy passion—I will do for that—
>   Alas, my God, I know not what.

Such a dying away in the last line is Herbert's way of
suggesting to his reader that the resources of language
have been overpast, what remains to be said can only be
stated with the utmost simplicity, as in the last line of
Dialogue when he has enumerated and attempted to com-
pete with all the sufferings of the Saviour:

> Ah no more: Thou break'st my heart,

or the last line of *Miserie* in which he has described the
folly and wickedness of man and ends with

> My God, I mean myself.

The first two words of the line are not an exclamation but
a vocative; it is in an entirely different key from the last
line of Hopkins' *Carrion Comfort*:

> That night, that year
> Of now done darkness I wretch lay wrestling with
>   (my God!) my God.

If Hopkins had written the last line of Herbert's *Miserie*
(if the fantasy may be allowed) it would have been an
exclamation of agonized discovery:

> (My God!)—I mean myself,

instead of as at present a quiet, humiliated recognition of the fact. In poem no. 45 (in Robert Bridges' edition) Hopkins considers the subject of Herbert's poem *Miserie*, the abject nature of mankind and therefore of himself: he closes his poem when the horror is at its height:

> I am gall, I am heartburn. God's most deep decree
>   Bitter would have me taste: my taste was me;
> Bones built in me, flesh filled, blood brimmed the curse,
>   Selfyeast of spirit a dull dough sours. I see
> The lost are like this, and their scourge to be
> As I am mine, their swetting selves; but worse.

Hopkins' sonnets are a crescendo of emotion, the strongest expression is reserved for the last line. Herbert, on the contrary, comes to rest on a note of quiet acceptance, some sentence that would be mere matter of fact, were it not for what has preceded. Yet the influence of Donne is conceivably present in either case; so differently can poets of different temperament make use of a common tradition. The best known and perhaps the most perfect of Herbert's poems, *Love* (III), will illustrate the measure of that difference.

> Love bade me welcome: yet my soul drew back,
>   Guiltie of dust and sinne.
> But quick-ey'd Love, observing me grow slack
>   From my first entrance in,
> Drew nearer to me, sweetly questioning,
>   If I lack'd any thing.
>
> A guest, I answer'd, worthy to be here:
>   Love said, You shall be he.
> I the unkinde, ungratefull? Ah my deare,
>   I cannot look on thee.
> Love took my hand, and smiling did reply,
>   Who made the eyes but I?

> Truth Lord, but I have marr'd them: let my shame
> > Go where it doth deserve.
> And know you not, sayes Love, who bore the blame?
> > My deare, then I will serve.
> You must sit down, sayes Love, and taste my meat:
> > So I did sit and eat.

No poem better represents the way in which Herbert assimilated and modified Donne's style. As so often with Donne, the plot of the poem is an argument, in this case a simple discussion between two protagonists. The relation between the soul and God is symbolized by a commonplace human situation, a travel-worn and shamefaced guest receiving hospitality. But Herbert, unlike Donne, develops his single situation at leisure and governs his reader's emotion almost entirely by his management of the tension. Starting at a low pitch he reaches the emotional climax in the middle of the poem:

> I the unkinde, ungratefull? Ah my deare,
> > I cannot look on thee.

and can then afford to relax gradually, completing his picture, but without emphasis; when the end is reached the emotion has become so poignant that the simple monosyllables in their prose order,

> So I did sit and eat.

convey more than the most impassioned rhetoric. All the feeling, that Herbert has so gradually and unostentatiously accumulated, rests upon the phrase. A graph might be made of the emotional plan of the poem in the shape of a pyramid; the two statements, "Love bade me welcome; yet my soul drew back," and "So I did sit and eat." are the bases upon which it rests; at the apex is the cry of self-disgust.

When he settled in the parsonage at Bemerton, Herbert did not cease to be the exquisite courtier whom

Walton so vividly describes. The same qualities of mind and temper found their outlet in poetry. In its sensitive modulations of tone we discern the master of social behaviour of whom Walton wrote that: "if during his lifetime he expressed any error, it was, that he kept himself at too great a distance with all his inferiors; and his clothes seemed to prove that he put too great a value on his parts and parentage"; and again, "the love of a court conversation, mixed with a laudable ambition to be something more than he was, drew him often to attend the king wheresoever the court was . . . he enjoyed his genteel humour for clothes, and court-like company, and seldom looked towards Cambridge unless the king were there, but then he never failed." The element of vanity in such a temperament, or of social snobbery he overcame (witness the anecdotes at the end of Walton's life as well as the evidence of the poetry itself);⁹ but the pic-

⁹ Walton tells us that Herbert went from time to time to Salisbury, to hear the Cathedral music and to "sing and play his part at an appointed private music-meeting." While walking to Salisbury on one such occasion, "he saw a poor man with a poorer horse, that was fallen under his load: they were both in distress, and needed present help; which Mr. Herbert perceiving, put off his canonical coat, and helped the poor man to unload, and after to load, his horse. The poor man blessed him for it, and he blessed the poor man; and was so like the Good Samaritan, that he gave him money to refresh both himself and his horse; and told him, 'that if he loved himself he should be merciful to his beast.' Thus he left the poor man: and at his coming to his musical friends at Salisbury, they began to wonder that Mr. George Herbert, which used to be so trim and clean, came into that company so soiled and discomposed: but he told them the occasion. And when one of the company told him 'He had disparaged himself by so dirty an employment,' his answer was, 'That the thought of what he had done would prove music to him at midnight; and that the omission of it would have upbraided and made discord in his conscience, whensoever he should pass by that place: for if I be bound to pray for all that be in distress, I am sure that I am bound, so far as it is in my power, to practise what I pray for. And though I do not wish for the like occasion every day, yet let me tell you, I would not willingly pass one day of my life without comforting a sad soul, or showing mercy; and I praise God for this occasion. And now let us tune our instruments.' "

ture sorts well with some of the most characteristic qualities of the poems. His perfect tact and delicate rendering of the changes of feeling or attitude, and above all his easy command of the right tone, without bluster, without self-consciousness: all this may well owe something to his breeding and his early intercourse.

CHAPTER V

Henry Vaughan

1622–1695

❦

> *The third requisite in our poet is imita-*
> *tion, to be able to convert the riches or*
> *substance of another poet to his own use.*
>   BEN JONSON

V AUGHAN was fascinated by the phrases of other poets. This is not unusual in a young poet; but the habit of borrowing continued with Vaughan to the end. At first his borrowings strike no roots, they are picked blossoms that have caught his fancy, later they are young shoots that bloom anew in his poems. In his two collections of secular poems, *Poems, with the Tenth Satire of Juvenal Englished* (1646) and *Olor Iscanus* (1651), the most obvious debts are to Donne and Habington, though he is attracted also by the Elizabethan use of mythological names and their Petrarchan attitude to the mistress. He seldom strikes a personal note; one suspects he is not sure of what he wants to say. His poems seem to fall apart, an elaborate image is followed by a lame conclusion. He is more interested in poetry than in his poem. In *Silex Scintillans* (1650), Herbert's influence is predominant. He rehandles Herbert's themes, borrows his phrases, copies his metrical effects, repeats his titles and yet now the poem is his own. Whatever he takes from Herbert he transmutes because his way of apprehending is different. The influence of Herbert's teaching, and probably other influences as well,[1] operated a "conversion" in Vaughan and he became a religious poet; but his religious experience was unlike Donne's or Herbert's and required for its expression different imagery and different rhythms.

Vaughan's indebtedness in his early volumes needs no elaborating. Mr. L. C. Martin, in his excellent edition (Clarendon Press, 1914), notes the various parallels. The fact that Vaughan borrows phrases, images or whole lines from his contemporaries is unimportant; it was the custom of the time. Donne's phrases are remodelled or even merely repeated in the poems of Carew, of Habington, of Suckling, of Godolphin and it is not surprising that Vaughan too made use of them, sometimes taking them direct from Donne himself, sometimes preferring the version of an imitator. But there are two peculiarities in these early poems. The first is that Vaughan never appears to be interested in his subject. He plays lovingly with an image and delays its application which is finally huddled into a last stanza. The other is that he prefers to draw his images from the countryside even when his model was Donne, who seldom looked in that direction. The result is often that his own experience, which finds an outlet in the image, has no inevitable connection with the situation to which he applies it with a logic more painstaking than convincing.

[1] Miss Elizabeth Holmes, in *Henry Vaughan and the Hermetic Philosophy* (Oxford, 1932), discusses the nature of these influences.

To AMORET, of the difference 'twixt him, and other
Lovers, and what true Love is.

Marke, when the Evenings cooler wings
 Fanne the afflicted ayre, how the faint Sunne,
  Leaving undone,
  What he begunne,
Those spurious flames suckt up from slime, and earth
  To their first, low birth,
  Resignes, and brings.

They shoot their tinsill beams, and vanities,
 Thredding with those false fires their way;
  But as you stay
  And see them stray,
You loose the flaming track, and subt'ly they
  Languish away,
  And cheate your Eyes.

Just so base, Sublunarie Lovers hearts
 Fed on loose prophane desires,
  May for an Eye,
  Or face comply:
But those removed, they will as soone depart,
  And shew their Art
  And painted fires.

Whilst I by pow'rfull Love, so much refin'd
 That my absent soule the same is
  Carelesse to misse,
  A glaunce, or kisse,
Can with those Elements of lust and sence,
  Freely dispence,
  And court the mind.

Thus to the North the Loadstones move,
 And thus to them th'enamour'd steel aspires:
  Thus, *Amoret,*
  I doe affect;

And thus by winged beames, and mutuall fire,
  Spirits and Stars conspire,
And this is LOVE.

In the first two stanzas he is describing an effect of
the evening light which he himself has noted: he has no
literary model, he is interested, and he dwells on more
detail than he can make use of for his parallel. There is
no convincing relation between the behaviour of light at
sunset and of "base, Sublunarie Lovers hearts"; they remain two separate observations arbitrarily linked together. He fares no better in the last stanza, into which
he crowds two more images, the already hackneyed load-
stone, and the image beloved by Donne of the stars in
their spheres governed by an "intelligence" or spirit.[2]
The total impression left by Vaughan's poem is that the
metaphysical conceit was, at this time, a fashion he accepted rather than the outcome of his own habit of mind.
He had not, like Donne, the kind of mind that is im-
mediately aware of logical situations recurring in diverse
kinds of experience; nor had he as yet, what he was to
discover later, a conception of the universe as a whole,
which would lead him to perceive a relation between its
various parts. There are signs in these early poems of the
direction in which Vaughan would look for such a conception. His poetry becomes sensitive and individual
when it describes nature, as it does nowhere else. He
dwells with loving particularly on scenes he has noted,
and especially on changes of light. A modern reader, wise
after the event, can recognize the poet of *The Dawning,
The Morning-watch, Midnight, The Search* and the
many more in which sunrise, sunset and starlight are
significant, when he reads such a poem as *To Amoret*

---

[2] Cf. *The Extasie* and *Aire and Angels*. The scholastic belief
which the image assumes is explained in Professor Grierson's
notes to these poems.

gone from Him with its sensitive, although half fanciful, description of the way in which the life fades out of a country scene at sunset:

> How the Spring
> That smil'd, and curl'd about his beames,
> Whilst he was here, now check'd her streames:
> The wanton Eddies of her face
> Were taught lesse noise, and smoother grace;
> And in a slow, sad channell went,
> Whisp'ring the banks their discontent:
> The carelesse ranks of flowers that spread
> Their perfum'd bosomes to his head,
> And with an open, free Embrace,
> Did entertaine his beamy face;
> Like absent friends point to the West,
> And on that weake reflection feast.

His secular poems, lacking as they do any individual outlook, only come to life when they reflect his responsiveness to the world about him. He looks even at nature partly through the eyes of other poets, but his own awareness and interest percolate through their phrases and fancies, even when he is writing complimentary verses, for instance: *To the best, and most accomplish'd Couple*—

> Fresh as the *houres* may all your pleasures be,
>   And healthfull as *Eternitie!*
> Sweet as the flowres *first breath,* and Close
> As th'*unseen spreadings* of the Rose,
> When he unfolds his Curtained head,
> And makes his bosome the *Suns bed,*

which, with its feeling for the secret, luxurious beauty of the rose, recalls Blake's *Sick Rose,* and Shelley's rose in *The Sensitive Plant*

Which unveiled the depth of her glowing breast
Till, fold after fold, to the fainting air
The soul of her beauty and love lay bare.

What was needed to make Vaughan a poet who stands
out from the contemporary galaxy of good versifiers, was
some central experience to which to relate his awareness
of nature. His poems became entities when he recognized
the phenomena of nature as relevant to his interpretation
of the world.

The main importance of Herbert's influence is that it
helped him to this end. Vaughan's preface to the second
edition of *Silex Scintillans* (1655) suggests that, whatever influences combined to make him a religious *man*,
Herbert was largely instrumental in making him a religious *poet*. Vaughan here dissociates himself from "those
ingenious persons, which in the late notion are termed
Wits," namely, those poets whom in his first two volumes
he had, almost slavishly, imitated "and here" he adds "because I would prevent a just *censure* by my free *confession*, I must remember, that I my self have, for many
years together, languished of this very *sickness*; and it is
no long time since I have recovered. But (blessed be God
for it!) I have by his saving assistance supprest my
greatest follies, and those which escaped from me, are (I
think) as innoxious, as most of that *vein* use to be; besides, they are interlin'd with many virtuous, and some
pious mixtures." Something had happened to make him
turn away with contempt from the amorous verse he had
so lately practised and he now claimed a new allegiance
to "that blessed man *Mr. George Herbert*, whose holy
life and *verse* gained many pious *Converts* (of whom I
am the least) and gave the first check to a most flourish-
ing and admired wit of his time."

Under Herbert's influence Vaughan discovered what
he really wanted to say. He was passionately concerned,

like Herbert himself, with the relation between God and the individual soul, and this concern increased and gave significance to his observations in the external world. When Vaughan began to explore his religious belief he found that it centred in his conception of nature. From being merely an ornament or an illustration his perceptiveness became the core of his poetry. Vaughan emerged from his contact with Herbert a metaphysical poet, not because Herbert was a metaphysical poet and he an imitative one, but because he now achieved a sense of direction and became capable of correlating his experiences. When he constructed his poems to _Amoret_ on the metaphysical plan, he was only an imitator. His arguments were ingenious elaborations of "occult resemblances." But in true metaphysical poetry the intellectual parallel, or the recondite image, expresses awareness of a world in which the separate and apparently unrelated parts strangely echo one another. They are suddenly seen in the poetry as facets of a single whole. So it is when Donne cries out to his weeping mistress:

> O more than Moone,
> Draw not up seas to drowne me in thy spheare,

or when, in _The Extasie_, he describes the relation between the self and the body:

> Wee are
> The intelligences, they the spheare.
> We owe them thankes, because they thus,
> Did us, to us, at first convay,
> Yeelded their forces, sense, to us,
> Nor are drosse to us, but allay.

Successful metaphysical imagery demands and repays close scrutiny. The meaning of the image tends to expand as we contemplate it, for instance in Donne's image of the moon his mistress is "more than Moone" because

she is more fair, more dear; because she draws the poet to
her as the moon the tides; because she draws up tears as
the moon will draw up the seas on which he is about to
voyage; and her tears are salt like the seas and like the
seas they may destroy him. All this and more is com-
pressed within the image. In false metaphysical poetry
the relation contemplated depends upon a one-sided and
superficial resemblance. Of such a kind is the predominant difference between Vaughan's secular poetry
and *Silex Scintillans.* He contemplates the same things,
sunset and starlight, birds and flowers; but, whereas before he looked round for a subject they could adorn and
contented himself with a partial relevance, they now
appear in the poetry as the terms in which he is thinking;
their relation to the subject is therefore intricate and
rich. The lingering light of evening, for instance, so
laboriously linked with the thought of his absent mistress
in *To Amoret gone from Him,* is now identified with the
effect upon his mind of the memory of the dead, the
relation seems as inevitable as it is rich in implications:

> They are all gone into the world of light!
>   And I alone sit lingring here;
> Their very memory is fair and bright,
>   And my sad thoughts doth clear.
>
> It glows and glitters in my cloudy brest
>   Like stars upon some gloomy grove,
> Or those faint beams in which this hill is drest,
>   After the Sun's remove.[3]

Herbert had little to teach Vaughan about the relation
between God and the created world. He himself contemplated God in the gospel story and in the forms and
ceremonies of the church. He seldom looked at the

[3] "They are all gone into the world of light!"

countryside; poems in which it figures are rare. There is the savour of first-hand enjoyment in *Easter*:

> I got me flowers to straw thy way;
> I got me boughs off many a tree:
> But thou wast up by break of day,
> And brought'st thy sweets along with thee.

And in *The Flower* he recognizes the kinship between the return of spring and the rhythmical recurrences of God's grace:

> How fresh, O Lord, how sweet and clean
> Are thy returns! ev'n as the flowers in spring;
> To which, besides their own demean,
> The last-past frosts tributes of pleasure bring.
> Grief melts away
> Like snow in May
> As if there were no such cold thing.

In *Easter-wings* the song and flight of the lark have been perceived as symbols. But these are exceptions in Herbert's work, whereas for Vaughan, after his "conversion,"

> all the vast expence
> In the Creation shed, and slav'd to sence
> Makes up but lectures for his eie, and ear.[4]

Nature for Vaughan is a revelation of the fulfilment of God's will. Herbert had envied her constancy; in his poem *Employment* (II) he exclaims,

> Oh that I were an Orenge-tree,
> That busie plant!
> Then should I ever laden be,
> And never want
> Some fruit for him that dressed me.

---

[4] *The Tempest.*

The "Orenge tree" which bears fruit and blossom at the same time was an apt illustration for his purpose. Vaughan looked nearer home and discerned in his immediate surroundings similar grounds for envy.

> I would I were a stone, or tree,
>   Or flowre by pedigree,
> Or some poor high-way herb, or Spring
>   To flow, or bird to sing!
> Then should I (tyed to one sure state,)
>   All day expect my date;
> But I am sadly loose, and stray
>   A giddy blast each way;
>   O let me not thus range!
>   Thou canst not change.[5]

Again, in *Rules and Lessons,* a poem profoundly influenced by Herbert as regards rhythm and structure, when he speaks of his favourite theme Vaughan is the loving observer of small sights and sounds, he bids man

> Walk with thy fellow-creatures: note the *hush*
> And *whispers* amongst them. There's not a *Spring*
> Or *Leafe* but hath his *Morning-hymn;* each *Bus*
> And *Oak* doth know *I AM;* canst thou not sing?

In *Christs Nativity,* bird song and starlight remind him of the difference between man and the rest of the creation:

> I would I were some *Bird,* or Star,
> Flutt'ring in woods, or lifted far
>   Above this *Inne*
>   And Rode of sin!
> Then either Star, or *Bird,* should be
> Shining, or singing still to thee.

[5] "And doe they so? have they a Sense."

In *Distraction,* starlight, rainbows and the radiance of
pearls are envied because, though they spend their light,
it does not diminish:

> Hadst thou
> Made me a starre, a pearle, or a rain-bow,
> The beames I then had shot
> My light had lessend not,
> But now
> I find my selfe the lesse, the more I grow;

Like Wordsworth, Vaughan is tempted to look back to
his childhood with regret, because to both poets it seemed
that children, like stars or flowers, fulfil the law of their
being unconsciously and inevitably. The thought expressed in Vaughan's *Retreate* is, as has often been pointed
out, similar in some respects to the thought in Wordsworth's *Intimations of Immortality;* this is due to an essential similarity in the outlook of the two poets. Both
believe in the creation as the expression of a single mind,
they turn to nature, not only to envy and admire, but
to discover. Nature is God's book; Wordsworth turns her
pages to find the prescriptions of that "Stern Daughter of
the voice of God" whom men call Duty:

> Stern Lawgiver! yet thou dost wear
> The Godhead's most benignant grace;
> Nor know we anything so fair
> As is the smile upon thy face:
> Flowers laugh before thee on their beds
> And fragrance in thy footing treads;
> Thou dost preserve the stars from wrong;
> And the most ancient heavens, through
>   Thee are fresh and strong.[6]

In the same spirit Vaughan contemplates the ordered
motions of the stars:

[6] *Ode to Duty.*

Fair, order'd lights (whose motion without noise
    Resembles those true Joys
Whose spring is on that hil where you do grow
    And we here tast sometimes below,)

With what exact obedience do you move
    Now beneath, and now above,
And in your vast progressions overlook
    The darkest night, and closest nook!

Some nights I see you in the gladsome East,
    Some others neer the West,
And when I cannot see, yet do you shine
    And beat about your endles line.

Silence, and light, and watchfulnes with you
    Attend and wind the Clue,
No sleep, nor sloth assailes you, but poor man
    Still either sleeps, or slips his span.[7]

Both poets expect to find in nature the secret of that

        something far more deeply interfused
    Whose dwelling is the light of setting suns
    And the round ocean, and the living air,
    And the blue sky, and in the mind of man:
    A motion and a spirit, that impels
    All thinking things, all objects of all thought,
    And rolls through all things.[8]

Several of Vaughan's contemporaries observed and enjoyed the world about them (Herrick for instance, and
Marvell, and Milton); but Vaughan's nature poetry is
different from theirs; he thinks of nature as a source of
revelation and could have said with Sir Thomas Browne:

"There are two Books from whence I collect my
Divinity; besides that written one of God, another of

---

[7] *The Constellation.*
[8] *Tintern Abbey.*

his servant Nature, that universal and publick Manuscript, that lies expans'd unto the Eyes of all: those that never saw him in the one, have discovered him in the other." [9]

Even for Traherne, who, among the poets of the century, approaches nearest to Vaughan's attitude, nature is rather a playground than an instructress; she is a delightful gift from God, rather than his interpreter:

> O hevenly Joy!
> O Great and Sacred Blessedness
> Which I possess!
> So great a Joy
> Who did into my Arms convey?

> From God abov
> Being sent, the gift doth me enflame
> To prais his Name;
> The Stars do mov,
> The Sun doth shine, to show his Lov.[1]

For Vaughan and later for Wordsworth nature shows not so much the love of God as his mind and meaning. Wordsworth tells us,

> As if awakened, summoned, roused, constrained,
> I looked for universal things; perused
> The common countenance of earth and sky:[2]

and Vaughan prays,

> O thou! whose spirit did at first inflame
> And warm the dead,
> And by a sacred Incubation fed
> With life this frame

[9] *Religio Medici* I xvi.
[1] Thomas Traherne, *Poems of Felicity, The Rapture.*
[2] *The Prelude,* Bk. III, ll. 109, 110.

> Which once had neither being, forme, nor name,
>   Grant I may so
> Thy steps track here below,
>
> That in these Masques and shadows I may see
>   Thy sacred way, . . .[3]

Vaughan observes and often closely imitates the workmanship of Herbert in *Silex Scintillans*, but this attitude
to the created world constantly affects his choice and use
of imagery. In a poem called *Affliction*, for instance, there
is every indication that he has been studying Herbert's
poetry, particularly the four poems with this same title,
as well as Herbert's *Deniall*. The theme is similar to that
of Herbert's *Affliction* (1). Both poets are contemplating
the suffering with which God purges his elect. The opening lines are in that staccato speech accent, which Herbert adapted from Donne:

> Peace, peace; It is not so. Thou doest miscall
>   Thy Physick; Pils that change
> Thy sick Accessions into setled health,
>   This is the great *Elixir* that turns gall
> To wine and sweetness; Poverty to wealth,
>   And brings man home, when he doth range.

The device, used by Herbert in *Deniall* and elsewhere, of
making an imperfect rhyme scheme reflect an inhar-
monious mood, is here adapted by Vaughan. He stresses
the irregularities of his metrical pattern until the end,
when it is regularized to represent the return of peace.
But the difference between Vaughan's poem and any of
Herbert's is far more essential than the resemblance.
Whereas Herbert may chance to draw a simile from nature, attaching no more importance to it than that it
affords the resemblance he requires:

[3] "I walkt the other day (to spend my hour,)."

> We are the trees whom shaking fastens more;

or

> Dissolve the knot
> As the sunne scatters by his light
> All the rebellions of the night;

Vaughan sees in such parallels a revelation of unity between the pattern of the world and the ordering of men's souls:

> Did not he, who ordain'd the day,
>   Ordain night too?
> And in the greater world display
> What in the lesser he would do?
> All flesh is Clay, thou know'st; and but that God
>   Doth use his rod,
> And by a fruitfull Change of frosts, and showres
>   Cherish, and bind thy *powr's*,
> Thou wouldst to weeds, and thistles quite disperse,
> And be more wild than is thy verse.
>
> .   .   .   .   .   .
>
> Were all the year one constant Sun-shine, wee
>   Should have no flowres,
> All would be drought, and leanness; not a tree
>   Would make us bowres;
>
> .   .   .   .   .
>
> Thus doth God *Key* disorder'd man
>   (Which none else can,)
> Tuning his brest to rise, or fall;
> And by a sacred, needfull art
> Like strings, stretch ev'ry part
> Making the whole most Musicall.[4]

Vaughan lays stress upon the repetition in the microcosm of the pattern of the macrocosm.

The Morning-watch, perhaps the most perfect whole among all Vaughan's poems (for he is often frag-

[4] *Affliction.*

mentary), seems to have developed out of a chance phrase of Herbert's. Herbert's poem, *Prayer* (1), is a rapid succession of similes; among other things prayer is likened to

> A kinde of tune which all things heare and fear.

Here is the poem which this line apparently suggested to Vaughan.

The Morning-watch

O Joyes! Infinite sweetnes! with what flowres,
And shoots of glory, my soul breakes, and buds!
   All the long houres
   Of night, and Rest
   Through the still shrouds
   Of sleep, and Clouds,
  This Dew fell on my Breast;
   O how it *Blouds*
And *Spirits* all my Earth! heark! In what Rings,
And *Hymning Circulations* the quick world
   Awakes, and sings;
   The rising winds,
   And falling springs,
   Birds, beasts, all things
  Adore him in their kinds.
   Thus all is hurl'd
In sacred *Hymnes,* and *Order,* The great *Chime*
And *Symphony* of nature. Prayer is
   The world in tune,
   A spirit-voyce,
   And vocall joyes
  Whose Echo is heav'ns blisse.
   O let me climbe
When I lye down! The Pious soul by night
Is like a clouded starre, whose beames though sed
   To shed their light
   Under some Cloud
   Yet are above

> And shine, and move
> Beyond that mistie shrowd.
>   So in my Bed
> That Curtain'd grave, though sleep, like ashes, hide
> My lamp, and life, both shall in thee abide.[5]

This is a very different way of recasting another poet's
phrase, from that exemplified in the *Lines to Amoret*.
The lines borrowed from Donne lost their original vigour
and gained nothing new from Vaughan's poem. But
Herbert's chance phrase is transformed into the focal
point of an apprehension of the world, which Herbert
had not developed and perhaps not thought of. His influence on Vaughan cannot be overstated in so far as it
directed him to the contemplation from which his poetry
was to spring; but it can be misstated if the wrong kind
of importance is attached to the verbal resemblances.
Herbert may have made Vaughan a poet, but he did not
make him in his own image. Vaughan is weak where
Herbert is strong, and strong where he is weak. He lacks
form, order, economy, he seldom knows where to stop;
whereas the perfection of form is characteristic of Herbert's poetry. On the other hand Vaughan has a gift of
song which Herbert often lacks. He can convey the

---

[5] In the lines "O how it Blouds . . . Hymning Circulations . . ." Vaughan combines the old and new physiology. Ac-
cording to the old belief, from the blood "spirits are first begotten
in the heart, which afterwards by the arteries are communicated
to the other parts" (Burton's *Anatomy of Melancholy*, Part I,
Sect. 1, Member II). Compare Donne's *The Extasie*, lines 61–
64, "As our blood labours to beget / Spirits, as like soules as it
can / Because such fingers need to knit / That subtile knot, which
makes us man. . . ." William Harvey's discovery of the circula-
tion of the blood was published in 1628. Vaughan, himself a
physician, would presumably have been interested. In these lines
both the blood-begotten vital spirits and the circular movement
of the blood represent the revitalizing of the poet and of the rest
of the created world, at dawn. Vaughan often italicizes words to
which he wants to draw the reader's attention, but no critic, as
far as I know, has especially attended to the relation between
Blouds-Spirits-Hymning Circulations.

ecstasy of joy or grief or worship by the movement of the verse, and he has a stronger instinct than Herbert for the magic of words and phrases. A selection of the best from Herbert would be a selection of poems, a selection of the best from Vaughan would include some single stanzas, lines, or even half lines.

Among these would be several that were suggested to him by Herbert. "Prayer is the world in tune" would need to be set in its context to convey all the meaning Vaughan perceived in it. Other phrases can be enjoyed in isolation. A phrase which to Herbert was only an essential part of the structure of a poem, was sometimes picked out by Vaughan and lovingly worked on till it satisfied his ear. Herbert had written, in a poem called *The Familie,*

> Joyes oft are there, and griefs as oft as joyes;
> > But griefs without a noise;
> Yet speak they louder then distemper'd fears.
> > What is so shrill as silent tears?

Vaughan, in *Olor Iscanus* (1651), in *An Epitaph upon the Lady Elizabeth,* made his first attempt to incorporate Herbert's phrase:

> Thy portion here was *griefe,* thy years
> Distilld no other rain, but tears,
> Tears without noise, but (understood)
> As lowd, and shrill as any bloud;

It was not very successful and the words still haunted him. In *Silex Scintillans,* in a poem called *Admission,* he found their final form:

> How shril are silent teares? . . .

It is the first half of a line of a poem which does not fulfil its promise; but the history of the line shows an interest in the choice and arrangement of words to produce an emotional impact. The magic of the phrase is Vaughan's, though it owes something to Herbert which is of vital importance. Vaughan learnt from Herbert the value of under-emphasis. He learnt to lead his reader on with commonplace words in a prose order until, all unprepared, he is brought up short by some startlingly poignant phrase. Instead of being first lifted out of the rut of triviality by the poet's emphasis and solemnity, he is shown the problems of life, death, time and eternity within the orbit of his daily experience. To speak familiarly of ultimate things is the prerogative of the metaphysical poets. Their habit of connecting the temporal and the eternal made it possible for them. It is not with any intention of avoiding the trivial that Vaughan most frequently expresses himself in terms of light and stars and running water; these were the stuff of his daily experience. He assimilated and adapted the manner of Herbert, which Herbert in turn had learnt from Donne. Without ceremony, as it were casually, these poets plunge us into the problems that baffle thought; so Donne,

> What if this present were the worlds last night?

or Herbert,

> Lord, how can man preach thy eternal word?

and Vaughan, in the same tradition, gives us,

> I saw Eternity the other night
> Like a great *Ring* of pure and endless light,
>   All calm, as it was bright,
> And round beneath it, Time in hours, days, years
>   Driv'n by the spheres
> Like a vast shadow mov'd, In which the world
>   And all her train were hurl'd; . . .⁶

⁶ *The World.*

Here is no imitation, but Vaughan has been able to as-
similate the influence of Donne, just as Herbert, with his
different outlook and temperament, had assimilated it.
The problem of time haunted Vaughan. Few poets have
phrased more beautifully the experience of time-bound
man striving to apprehend eternity; or of the bewildering
variation in the rate at which time passes:

> Silence, and stealth of dayes! 'Tis now
> > Since thou art gone,
> Twelve hundred houres . . .

is the opening of a poem about the death of his brother.
For Vaughan, as for Donne, the "houres, dayes, moneths,
which are the rags of time,"

> Heav'n
> Is a plain watch and without figures winds
> All ages up; who drew this Circle even
> > He fils it; Dayes, and hours are *Blinds*.[7]

Donne's influence over this school of poetry was very
great; but each of his followers who deserves separate
attention contributed something of his own to the tradition. Vaughan brought a new range of experience within
the compass of this style. No one else among Donne's
followers watched the earth, sky, and water, the birds and
flowers with the same emotion, nor with the same deli-
cacy of observation. Vaughan lacked Donne's vigorous
and varied awareness of human character and affairs; he
lacked Herbert's sobriety and exquisite sense of form,
his undeviating control of powerful feeling; but often his
poetry has a radiance and a movement which neither of
these attempts. Vaughan, who resembles Wordsworth in
his nature mysticism, sometimes resembles Shelley in the
ecstatic outpouring of his numbers. He is more lyrical

---

[7] *The Evening-watch. A Dialogue.*

than his masters. Perhaps he is less restrained by intellectual perplexity. He could immerse himself in rapturous contemplation of dawn or sunset. Neither Donne nor Herbert could have written *The Dawning:* but Vaughan would not have written it as he did had he not learnt from them and assimilated the metaphysical influence. It is a song of rapture, but with an intellectual ground base.

Ah! what time wilt thou come? when shall that crie
  The *Bridegroome's Comming!* fil the sky?
  Shall it in the Evening run
  When our words and works are done?
  Or wil thy all-surprizing light
    Break at midnight?
  When either sleep, or some dark pleasure
  Possesseth mad man without measure;
  Or shal these early, fragrant hours
    Unlock thy bowres?
  And with their blush of light descry
  Thy locks crown'd with eternitie;
  Indeed, it is the only time
  That with thy glory doth best chime,
  All now are stirring, ev'ry field
    Ful hymns doth yield,
  The whole Creation shakes off night,
  And for thy shadow looks the light,
  Stars now vanish without number,
  Sleepie Planets set, and slumber,
  The pursie Clouds disband, and scatter,
  All except some sudden matter,
  Not one beam triumphs, but from far
    That morning-star.

From first to last Vaughan laid himself open to the influence of other poets, but he emerged with a way of perceiving and of expressing his perceptions which bore his own hallmark.

CHAPTER VI

Richard Crashaw

1613?–1649

That our sensuality by the vertue of Christ's Passion, be brought up into the substance.

CRESSY,
Revelation of Divine Love

IN so far as we read poetry to discover what the poet meant, as much as, or at least as well as, what his poem may mean to us, his biography is a useful crutch. We know little of Crashaw's life beyond the bare outline; but that little helps us to envisage the man who wrote the poems. His mother died when he was a baby, the exact date is unknown, but he had a step-mother by the time he was seven years old, and she died a year later. During that brief space we are told that she showed a "singular motherly affection for the child of her predecessor." Other women befriended him when he grew up. He speaks with warm and reverent affection of the Mother of a Community, who was possibly Mary Collet, the niece of Nicholas Ferrar of Little Gidding; she is described by him, in a letter, as "the gentlest, kindest, most tender-hearted and liberall handed soul I think this day alive." The Countess of Denbigh and Queen Henrietta

Maria were good to him and recommended him for preferment at Rome; but he was never to find

> That not impossible shee
> That shall command my heart and mee;[1]

and the fact that he was appointed to a College Fellow-
ship in 1635 (when he was twenty-two years old), and
that he continued to prefer the monastic life, "a little
contentfull kingdom" as he describes it, suggests that he
never seriously sought her. For Crashaw, as for Herbert,
religion supplied the only outlet for an emotional nature.
Yet the two poets were so different in temperament that,
although both wrote love poems to God and both were
influenced in some degree by the prevailing poetic fashion, their poetry has little in common.

Crashaw's father, William Crashaw, was a puritan
parson, and wrote anti-papal pamphlets of some violence.
It has been suggested that Crashaw's own Roman leanings were due to a reaction from parental authority; but
as his father, who died when Richard was only thirteen,
was a man of sufficiently catholic sympathies to translate
Jesuit hymns to the Virgin from "the most mistie times
of Popery," it seems on the whole more likely that Crashaw inherited from his father the temperament that led
him first to Laudian high-churchmanship, and finally to
Roman Catholicism.

The boy was sent to the Charterhouse School after his
father's death and from thence to Pembroke College,
Cambridge, as an Exhibitioner, in 1631. Almost at once
he began to write elegies in English and Latin. It is im-
probable that he felt much for the deaths of Dr. Samuel
Brooke or Dr. Mansell; they merely provided him with an
opportunity to exercise his talent. The death of Michael
Chambers, a young Fellow of Queens', and of "the most

---

[1] *Wishes. To his (supposed) Mistresse.*

desired Mr. Herrys," Fellow of Pembroke, are in a different case. These two were akin to him in their youthfulness and in their service of the muses. They were in much the same relation to him as Henry King was to Milton, and Crashaw, like Milton, dwells on the frustrated hopes of those who had expected their talents to bear fruit:

> For Life by volumes lengthened
> A Line or two, to speake him dead.
> For the Laurell in his verse,
> The sullen Cypresse o're his Herse.
> For a silver-crowned Head
> A durty pillow in Death's Bed.
> For so deare, so deep a trust,
> Sad requitall, thus much dust! [2]

He wrote five poems inspired by the death of Herrys and there are lines in each of them that foreshadow his maturer poetry. They display his propensity for nursing an emotion and savouring all the sweetness of grief, and they show also Crashaw's habit of worrying out of his conceits their emotional and sensational, rather than their intellectual, implications:

> The fresh hopes of his lovely Youth,
> Flourisht in so faire a grouth.
> So sweet the Temple was, that shrin'd
> The Sacred sweetnesse of his mind.
> That could the Fates know to relent?
> Could they know what mercy meant;
> Or had ever learnt to beare,
> The soft tincture of a Teare:
> Teares would now have flow'd so deepe,
> As might have taught Griefe how to weepe.
> Now all their steely operation,
> Would quite have lost the cruell fashion.

[2] *Upon the Death of a Gentleman.*

> Sicknesse would have gladly been,
> Sick himself to have sav'd him:
> And his Feaver wish'd to prove
> Burning, onely in his Love.[3]

The last image inevitably suggests a comparison with Donne's impassioned intellectual paradoxes in *A Feaver*, and especially with the stanza in which he recognizes the fever as a like-minded rival:

> Yet 'twas of my minde, seizing thee,
>   Though it in thee cannot persever.
> For I had rather owner bee
>   Of thee one houre, than all else ever.

But the difference between the two poets in their handling of the conceit is far more striking than their resemblance in its conception. Crashaw slowly elaborates an hypothesis, he has time to dwell on the sweetness of the mind and of the body that enshrined it, to picture the "soft" tears of the Fates, the weeping of Sorrow, the sickness of Sickness and the burning love of Feaver, while Donne rushes from one intellectual hyperbole to another including, as is his habit, a wide range of speculation within the single experience:

> O wrangling schooles, that search what fire
>   Shall burne this world, had none the wit
> Unto this knowledge to aspire,
>   That this her feaver might be it?
>
> And yet shee cannot wast by this,
>   Nor long beare this torturing wrong,
> For much corruption needfull is
>   To fuell such a feaver long.

The conceit of the Feaver as a lover is only one of a series of situations that Donne invents, in order to de-

---

[3] *Another* (on the death of Mr. Herrys).

velop his hypothesis that his mistress cannot die. The Feaver can only enjoy his love for a moment because

> much corruption needfull is
> To fuell such a feaver long,

therefore

> These burning fits but meteors bee,
> Whose matter in thee is soone spent,

and from this again it follows logically that the "feever" must be of the same mind as the poet and prefer to enjoy her, though it be only for a moment. In Crashaw's poem there is no logical chain of connection, but only a succession of emotional scenes.

These elegies were not the only poems Crashaw wrote at Pembroke; his lines *Upon the gunpowder treason*, while they demonstrate that he was not as yet conscious of Roman Catholic sympathies, display also another aspect of the sensationalism which was to remain an outstanding characteristic of his poetry:

> Grow plumpe, leane Death; his Holinesse a feast
> Hath now praepar'd, & you must be his guest.
> Come grimme destruction. & in purple gore
> Dye seu'n times deeper then they were before
> Thy scarlet robes. for heer you must not share
> A common banquett, noe, heere's princely fare.
>
> .   .   .   .
>
> But dares destruction eate these candid breasts,
> The Muses, & the Graces sugred neasts? [4]
> Dares hungry death snatch of one cherry lipp?
> Or thirsty treason offer once to sippe
> One dropp of this pure Nectar, which doth flow
> In azure channells warme through mounts of snow?
>
> .   .   .   .

[4] The nature of the pun here, while it is in the fashion of the time, is peculiarly to Crashaw's own taste.

Poore meagre horror streightwaies was amaz'd
And in the stead of feeding stood, & gaz'd.
Their appetites were gone at th' uery sight;
But yet their eyes surfett with sweet delight.
Only the Pope a stomack still could find;
But yett they were not powder'd to his mind.

It may seem unfair to dwell upon so early and so crude a poem, and one which Crashaw would have repudiated later for its sentiments. But its faults are of a kind that he never outgrew and that differentiate him sharply from Donne and from Donne's imitators. Whereas they tend to over-elaborate an idea, Crashaw loves to elaborate sensations. Moreover, his sensations are peculiar and sometimes repellent. The collocation of torture and erotic emotion in this poem is of a kind that occurs repeatedly in Crashaw's poetry from first to last. There can be no doubt that the conjunction of physical torture with sensual love was to him pleasurable and inevitable; compare for instance the third and fourth stanzas of *On the wounds of our crucified Lord*.

O thou that on this foot hast laid
    Many a kisse, and many a Teare,
Now thou shal't have all repaid,
    Whatsoe're thy charges were.

This foot hath got a Mouth and lippes,
    To pay the sweet summe of thy kisses:
To pay thy Teares, an Eye that weeps
    In stead of Teares such Gems as this is.

In such ways as these Crashaw's early College poems foretell the future characteristics of his verse and mark the lines along which he was to diverge from the Donne tradition.

There is no evidence of Roman Catholic leanings during his years at Cambridge but he was throughout under the influence of the high Church and Royalist party and he was, as we should expect, particularly interested in a decorative, ritualistic form of worship. He wrote complimentary verses to Laney, the Master of Pembroke, praising him for restoring the beauty of the College chapel and its worship, and also to his tutor Tournay, who was refused the degree of B.D. for impugning the puritan doctrine of justification by faith, and in about the year 1635 Crashaw moved over from Pembroke to Peterhouse, which was then the centre of Laudian high-churchmanship. Here he seems to have been actively concerned in decorating the new chapel and also to have been noted for his ascetic devotions in the church of Little St. Mary's, which served as Peterhouse Chapel until the new one was ready:

> There he made his nest more gladly then David's Swallow neere the house of God: where like a primitive Saint, he offered more prayers in the night, then others usually offer in the day.[5]

He remained at Peterhouse until 1643 and there two poets were his friends, Joseph Beaumont, Fellow of Peterhouse from 1636–44, and Cowley, who came up in 1637. Neither of these seems to have influenced his poetry very much, it was of far greater importance that during these years he acquired the Spanish and Italian languages. This meant that he could read the Spanish mystics and the biographies of the recently canonized Saint Teresa (canonized in 1622) and that he could steep himself in the "hyperboles and luscious sweetness of the Italian poet Marino." These are the influences that are most manifest upon the thought and style of his poetry and that in part account for its deviation from any

---

[5] *Steps to the Temple.* The Preface to the Reader, 1648.

of the dominant schools of poetry in the England of his day.

Crashaw enjoyed eight years of peaceful study and contemplation at Peterhouse, but by 1643 Cambridge had become uninhabitable for a high-churchman and a Royalist. Cosin, the Master of Peterhouse, was expelled for sending the College plate to the king at York in 1643, and in the same year Crashaw was at Leyden from whence he wrote a long letter to a friend at Cambridge. The main purpose of the letter was to make arrangements whereby he might one day hope to return to Peterhouse for, he writes,

> I haue I assure you no desire to be absolutely and ir-respectiuely rid of my beloued Patrimony in St. Peter. No man then myself holds more high the humble sceptre of such a little contenfull kingdom. And as safely may I say no man more unprouided of any present course.

But there was to be no return. Crashaw's movements in the next few years cannot be certainly known. It is probable that he went for a time to Oxford, where the court had been established. If so he would there have become acquainted with the Countess of Denbigh to whom he dedicated the revised edition of his sacred poems, *Carmen Deo Nostro:*

> To my Lady the Covntesse of Denbigh by her most devoted servant. R.C. In hearty acknowledgment of his immortall obligation to her Goodnes & Charity.

Here also he would have met his other protectress, Queen Henrietta Maria.

But all this is conjectural. The next time Crashaw is referred to in contemporary documents after the letter from Leyden, is in a letter from his friend Cowley.

Cowley crossed over to France in 1646 as secretary to
Lord Jermyn, the minister in attendance on Queen Henrietta Maria. He found Crashaw in Paris "being a meere
scholar and very shiftless" and it may have been he who
recommended him to the notice of the queen. Crashaw's
conversion to Roman Catholicism must have taken place
during the obscure years in his biography between 1643
and 1646, since his *Steps to the Temple* published in
1646 contains the apology for the Hymn to St. Teresa
"being written while he was yet among the protestants."
In 1646 the queen wrote a letter recommending Crashaw
to the care of the Pope and with it he set out for Rome.
There was some delay during which Crashaw's poverty
was unrelieved and then, in 1647, he was found by Dr.
John Bargrave in the service of Cardinal Palotto. Bargrave gives an account of the last three years of Crashaw's
life:

> When I went first of my four times to Rome there
> were four revolters to the Roman Church that had been
> fellows of Peterhouse in Cambridge with myself. The
> name of one of them was Mr. R. Crashaw who was
> . . . one of the followers of this Cardinal. . . . Mr.
> Crashaw infinitely commended his Cardinal but com-
> plained extremely of the wickedness of those of his
> retinue of which he, having the Cardinal's ear, com-
> plained to him. Upon which the Italians fell so far out
> with him that the Cardinal, to secure his life, was fain
> to put him from his service, and procuring him some
> small imploy at the Lady's of Loretto; whither he went
> in pilgrimmage in summer time, and, overheating him-
> self died in four weeks after he came thither, and it
> was doubtful whether he were not poisoned.

From these sparse events and from the few contemporary references to Crashaw, we see him as a man of
rare single-mindedness. He continually directed himself

towards a mode of life which would afford him peace and
leisure for contemplation. The world did not tempt him.
Severed from the shelter of his College Chapel and of
friends like-minded with himself, he sought the protection and support of the Roman Catholic Church. He
seems always to have starved himself of bodily comfort
and to have cared only for comfort of the spirit. His
friends thought him indifferent to all that the world has
to offer. Thomas Car, in verses introducing the first edition of *Carmen Deo Nostro*, 1652, describes him for us:

> To witt, being pleas'd with all things, he pleas'd all;
> Nor would he giue, nor take offence; befall
> What might; he would possesse himselfe: and liue
> As deade (deuoyde of interest) t'all might giue
> Desease t'his well-composed mynd, forestal'd
> With heauenly riches, which had wholy call'd
> His thoughtes from earth, to liue aboue in'th air,
> A very bird of paradice. No care
> Had he of earthly trashe. What might suffice
> To fitt his soule to heauenly exercise
> Sufficed him; and may we guesse his hart
> By what his lipps brings forth, his onely part
> Is God and godly thoughtes. Leaues doubt to none
> But that to him one God is all; all's one.
> What he might eate or weare he tooke no thought;
> His needfull foode he rather found then sought.
> He seekes no downes, no sheetes, his bed's still made;
> If he can find a chaire or stoole, he's layd;
> When day peepes in, he quitts his restlesse rest,
> And still, poore soul, before he's vp he's dres't.

. . . . .

From the time he left Cambridge he was miserably poor,
except for the few years under Palotto's protection, and
this he sacrificed because he would not tolerate the
"wickedness" of his fellow-attendants. The sole satisfac-

tion he allowed to his sensual and emotional needs was
poetry, and in his poetry the senses and the emotions
had their revenge.

When Crashaw turns to poetry his attention fixes itself
on the particular sensation he contemplates. The poem
On the wounds of our crucified Lord, already quoted,
may seem an extreme example; but the treatment of the
theme is typical of Crashaw's method. He dwells on the
actual wounds and their texture and seeks to communicate the horror and pity of the particular moment. Herbert handles the same theme in *Good Friday;* but in him
it arouses a series of thoughts instead of a series of sensual
and emotional impressions:

> Shall I thy woes
> Number according to thy foes?
> Or, since one starre show'd thy first breath,
>   Shall all thy death?
>
> Or shall each leaf
> Which falls in Autumne, score a grief?
> Or can not leaves, but fruit, be signe
>   Of the true vine?

This is poetry learnt in the school of Donne, in which a
conceit is the starting point of cogitation. The same kind
of comparison can be drawn between Crashaw's *The
Weeper* and either Donne's *A Valediction: of weeping*
or Marvell's *Eyes and Tears.* For Donne and for Marvell
the visual image of the tear suggests a series of thoughts
logically connected with the shape, texture or behaviour
of tears. But in Crashaw's poem one sensual image gives
rise only to another. The senses remain dominant; if we
move away from the tears of the Magdalene it is not to
some thought they suggest, some generalization about the
nature of love or sorrow, but to another image which has
for Crashaw the same tender sweetness:

The dew no more will weepe,
The Primroses pale cheeke to decke,
The deaw no more will sleepe,
Nuzzel'd in the Lillies necke.
Much rather would it tremble heere,
And leave them both to bee thy Teare.

Not the soft Gold which
Steales from the Amber-weeping Tree,
Makes sorrow halfe so Rich,
As the drops distil'd from thee.
Sorrowes best Iewels lye in these
Caskets, of which Heaven keeps the Keyes.

When sorrow would be seene
In her brightest Majesty,
(For shee is a Queen)
Then is shee drest by none but thee.
Then, and onely then shee weares
Her richest Pearles, I meane thy Teares.

Not in the Evenings Eyes
When they red with weeping are,
For the Sun that dyes,
Sits sorrow with a face so faire.
Nowhere but heere did ever meet
Sweetnesse so sad, sadnes so sweet.

The nestling image in the first stanza,

The deaw no more will sleepe
Nuzzel'd in the Lillies necke,

brings to the mind a procession of similar images in
Crashaw's poetry, images of nests and other soft secret
refuges, in which shelter, warmth and sweetness are
found. In the poem *To the Name above every Name,
the Name of Jesus,* the word "nest" occurs five times,
with this meaning more or less explicit; the following are
two typical examples:

All ye wise SOVLES, who in the wealthy Brest
Of this vnbounded NAME build your warm Nest.

                                                    ll. 11, 12.

Our Murmurs haue their Musick too,
Ye mighty ORBES, as well as you;
    Nor yeilds the noblest Nest
Of warbling SERAPHIM to the eares of Loue,
A choicer Lesson then the ioyfull BREST
    Of a poor panting Turtle-Doue.

                                                    ll. 103 ff.

It will be noticed here and elsewhere in Crashaw's poetry
that the words nest and breast or bosom are closely associated, they are alternate symbols of protection and fostering love. In *Sancta Maria Dolorum* he writes,

> O Mother turtle-doue!
> Soft sourse of love
> That these dry lidds might borrow
> Somthing from thy full Seas of sorrow!
> O in that brest
> Of thine (the noblest nest
> Both of loue's fires & flouds) might I recline
> This hard, cold, Heart of mine!

In the nativity hymn the chorus of Angels sings,

> We saw thee in thy baulmy Nest,
> Young dawn of our aeternal Day! [6]

But the meaning that nestling imagery has for Crashaw
is perhaps most fully brought out in the second stanza or
Vexilla Regis. The Hymn of the Holy Crosse:

> Lo, how the streames of life, from that full nest
> Of loues, thy lord's too liberall brest,
> Flow in an amorous floud

---

[6] *In the Holy Nativity of our Lord God. A Hymn sung as by
the Shepherds*, ll. 31–2.

Of WATER wedding BLOOD.
With these he wash't thy stain, transfer'd thy smart,
And took it home to his own heart.

To return to the stanzas of *The Weeper* which gave rise
to this digression. Crashaw succeeds, in the stanzas
quoted, in expressing the particular quality of emotion
he experiences in contemplating the Magdalene. In them
he develops a picture of delicate, grave, queenly sorrow,
enviable in its utter abandon. Other stanzas which pre-
cede and follow it in the poem are less successful and
have been deservedly ridiculed, for example, stanzas
4 and 5:

> Vpwards thou dost weep.
> Heaun's bosome drinks the gentle stream.
> Where th'milky riuers creep,
> Thine floates aboue; & is the cream.
> Waters aboue th'Heauns, what they be
> We'are taught best by thy TEARES & thee.

> Euery morn from hence
> A brisk Cherub somthing sippes
> Whose sacred influence
> Addes sweetnes to his sweetest Lippes.
> Then to his musick. And his song
> Tasts of this Breakfast all day long.

It is not merely our own commonplace associations
with, for instance, the word breakfast, that makes the
stanzas unacceptable; it is Crashaw's mercilessly minute
dwelling on sensations, unrelated to thought. The same
fault is to be found with his unnecessarily concrete development of an image (which he added to the poem
when he revised it) of the Magdalene's eyes as

> Two walking baths; two weeping motions;
> Portable, & compendious oceans.

It is doubtful whether a poet in whom the senses and the emotions were so much more active than the intellect, was well served by the metaphysical style.

The metaphysical conceit at its most effective is a focal point at which emotion, sense-impression and thought are perceived as one. Sense-impression is controlled and limited by the context; for instance, in the second stanza of Donne's *Funerall,*

> For if the sinewie thread my braine lets fall
> > Through every part,
> Can tye those parts, and make mee one of all;
> These haires which upward grew, and strength and art
> > Have from a better braine,
> Can better do'it . . .

The connection between the "sinewie thread" or spinal cord, centre of the nervous system, and "those haires which upward grew" is perceived by the intellect; it is, and this is not uncommon with Donne, rather impeded than otherwise by strong visual imagery; what the reader perceives is more a diagram than a picture. Sometimes, on the other hand, a metaphysical conceit demands a response from the senses and the intellect, but makes no impact on the emotions; for instance, Donne's conceit in *Communitie,*

> But they are ours as fruits are ours,
> He that but tasts, he that devours,
> > And he that leaves all, doth as well:
> Chang'd loves are but chang'd sorts of meat,
> And when hee hath the kernell eate,
> > Who doth not fling away the shell?

But the element that is always present and that distinguishes Donne's conceits and those of his followers from other types of conceit, is the intellectual element.

For Donne such an instrument was peculiarly apt and necessary. His mind was constantly spurred to fresh activity by sensation or by emotion, and the total experience resulting could only be conveyed in the metaphysical conceit. Herbert made more sparing use of it; but at times a conceit of this nature enabled him to pass from description or analysis to synthesis. For instance, in the poem *Content,* where he describes and meditates about the contented soul, his contemplation culminates in a series of conceits in which the thought is identified with sensations and their corresponding emotions:

> This soul doth span the world, and hang content
> From either pole unto the centre;
> Where in each room of the well-furnisht tent
> He lies warm and without adventure.
>
> The brags of life are but a nine dayes wonder;
> And after death the fumes that spring
> From private bodies make as big a thunder
> As those which rise from a huge King.
>
> Onely thy Chronicle is lost; and yet
> Better by worms be all once spent
> Then to have hellish moths still gnaw and fret
> Thy name in books, which may not rent:
>
> When all thy deeds, whose brunt thou feel'st alone,
> Are chaw'd by others pens and tongue;
> And as their wit is, their digestion,
> Thy nourisht fame is weak or strong.

The attitude here adopted was the consequence of thought and the logic of the images continues the activity which gave rise to them. Crashaw's images, on the other hand, arise directly out of his emotional needs. A passage from *To the Name above every Name, the Name of Jesus,* will illustrate the difference:

Little, alas, thought They
Who tore the Fair Brests of thy Friends,
    Their Fury but made way
For Thee; And seru'd therein Thy glorious ends.
What did Their weapons but with wider pores
Inlarge thy flaming-brested Louers
        More freely to transpire
        That impatient Fire
The Heart that hides Thee hardly couers.
What did their Weapons but sett wide the Doores
For Thee: Fair, purple Doores, of loue's deuising;
The Ruby windowes which inrich't the East
Of Thy so oft repeated Rising.
Each wound of Theirs was Thy new Morning;
And reinthron'd thee in thy Rosy Nest,
With blush of thine own Blood thy day adorning,
It was the witt of loue o'reflowd the Bounds
Of Wrath, & made thee way through All Those
        Wounds.

These conceits are undoubtedly focal points of Crashaw's
experience; but what elements are united in them? Their
elements are sensations and emotions. Yet, in a sense,
they are metaphysical, for it is the intellect that operates
the union. It is by a logical device that he unites in them
the sensation of love and the sensation of pain. This is
the peculiarity of his conceits, sharply differentiating
them from those of Donne, Herbert or Vaughan. The intellect is operative, not before or after, but only in the
moment of apprehending the image. By its means he con-
trives images which satisfy his emotional needs. The
images of the ascetic Crashaw are far more predomi-
nantly sexual than those of Donne, who had known the
pleasures of sensuality, or of Herbert, who never seems
to have desired them. He constantly identifies the processes of conception, birth and fostering, with the love
that unites God and the saints. The function of the in-

tellect in his poetry is to give logical coherence to his
perception of identity between these things. What is
meant can be made plain by a series of examples. The
first is from the poem just quoted. He is addressing the
dawn of that day which is to bring the name of Christ
to earth:

> Lo where it comes, vpon The snowy Dove's
> Soft Back; And brings a Bosom big with Loues.
> Welcome to our dark world, Thou
>   Womb of Day!
> Vnfold thy fair Conceptions; And display
> The Birth of our Bright Ioyes.

A similar conceit is developed in the first stanza of *Easter
Day*:

> Rise, Heire of fresh Eternity,
>   From thy Virgin Tombe:
> Rise mighty man of wonders, and thy world with thee
>   Thy Tombe, the universall East,
>   Natures new wombe,
> Thy Tombe, faire Immortalities perfumed Nest.

In the last stanza of *The Hymn of Sainte Thomas in
Adoration of the Blessed Sacrament* he develops the parallel between God's love for man and maternal love, the
source of nourishment. The image here is not of suckling
at the breast but of the sacrificial nourishing attributed
to the pelican, by means of which Crashaw is again able
to identify love and physical pain:

>   O soft self-wounding Pelican!
> Whose brest weepes Balm for wounded man.
> Ah this way bend thy benign floud
> To'a bleeding Heart that gaspes for blood.
> That blood, whose least drops soueraign be
> To wash my worlds of sins from me.
> Come love! Come Lord! & that long day

> For which I languish, come away.
> When this dry soul those eyes shall see,
> And drink the vnseal'd sourse of thee.
> When Glory's sun faith's shades shall chase,
> And for thy veil giue me thy FACE.

The conceits in all three instances are metaphysical in so far as they depend upon logical connections; reasoned analysis brings out their full meaning. But the function of the intellect in Crashaw's poetry is to justify an unusual collocation of sensations.

A Hymn to The Name and Honor of the Admirable Sainte Teresa is the poem of Crashaw's which has rightly attracted most readers. It is <u>his most complete and adequate expression</u> of his own religious experience. In it he makes little use of intellectual conceits because he had little need for them. The theme itself involved the conjunction of feelings that most moved him. He had only to tell his story and, in the telling, to convey what it meant to him:

> Love, thou art Absolute sole lord
> Of LIFE & DEATH. To proue the word,
> Wee'l now appeal to none of all
> Those thy old Souldiers, Great & tall,
> Ripe Men of Martyrdom, that could reach down
> With strong armes, their triumphant crown;
> Such as could with lusty breath
> Speak lowd into the face of death
> Their Great LORD's glorious name, to none
> Of those whose spatious Bosomes spread a throne
> For LOVE at larg to fill: spare blood & sweat;
> And see him take a priuate seat,
> Making his mansion in the mild
> And milky soul of a soft child.
>
>   Scarse had she learn't to lisp the name
> Of Martyr; yet she thinks it shame
> Life should so long play with that breath

Which spent can buy so braue a death.
She neuer vndertook to know
What death with loue should haue to doe;
Nor has she e're yet vnderstood
Why to show loue, she should shed blood
Yet though she cannot tell you why,
She can LOVE, & she can DY.

It is in this poem that Crashaw best succeeds in com-
municating to his reader his own attitude towards martyrdom, an attitude not merely of admiration but of envy.
It is the luxury of pain that we feel in the lines:

O how oft shalt thou complain
Of a sweet & subtle PAIN.
Of intolerable IOYES;
Of a DEATH, in which who dyes
Loues his death, and dyes again.
And would for euer so be slain.
And liues, & dyes; and knowes not why
To liue, But that he thus may neuer leaue to DY.

The consummation of her martyrdom he can best express
in terms of consummated love:

O what delight, when reueal'd LIFE shall stand
And teach thy lipps heav'n with his hand;
On which thou now maist to thy wishes
Heap up thy consecrated kisses.

. . . . .

Thou shalt look round about, & see
Thousands of crown'd Soules throng to be
Themselues thy crown. Sons of thy vowes
The virgin-births with which thy souereign spouse
Made fruitfull thy fair soul,

Crashaw wrote two more poems inspired by Saint Teresa,
*An Apologie for the Fore-going Hymne as having been
writt when the author was yet among the protestantes*

and _The Flaming Heart upon the Book and Picture of the Seraphicall Saint Teresa_. Neither of these is as sustained a lyrical outburst as the first; but in the closing lines of the last poem the harmony of theme, mood and manner are once more perfectly achieved. They are the loveliest lines Crashaw ever wrote and perhaps the lines in which he most easily and fully expressed himself. They raise once more the question whether the peculiar qualities of Donne's style: intellectual imagery, logical forms and speech rhythms, were of any service to Crashaw. Was he not at his best when he least needed or employed them; when, as here, he could dispense with the intricacies of the conceit and "pour out his full heart"?

> O thou vndanted daughter of desires!
> By all thy dowr of LIGHTS & FIRES;
> By all the eagle in thee, all the doue;
> By all thy liues & deaths of loue;
> By thy larg draughts of intellectuall day,
> And by thy thirsts of loue more large then they;
> By all thy brim-fill'd Bowles of feirce desire,
> By thy last Morning's draught of liquid fire;
> By the full kingdome of that finall kisse
> That seiz'd thy parting Soul, & seal'd thee his;
> By all the heau'ns thou hast in him
> (Fair sister of the SERAPHIM!)
> By all of HIM we haue in THEE;
> Leaue nothing of my SELF in me.
> Let me so read thy life, that I
> Vnto all life of mine may dy.[7]

[7] _The Flaming Heart upon the Book and Picture of the Seraphicall Saint Teresa._

CHAPTER VII

Religious Poetry: A Postscript

> *Contemplative piety, or the intercourse be-*
> *tween God and the human soul, cannot be*
> *poetical.*
>
> DR. JOHNSON,
> *Life of Waller*

THE poets to whom Donne's influence was most con-
genial were religious poets. Conceits reminiscent
of his and poems influenced by his conception of
structure and rhythm are common in the love poetry of
the day; but, when one examines them more closely, the
likeness to Donne proves often to be superficial:

Excuse of Absence.

You will not ask, perhaps, wherefore I stay,
Loving so much, so long away—
O do not think 'twas I did part,
It was my body, not my heart;
For, like a compass, on your love
One foot is fix'd, and cannot move:
Th'other may follow the blind guide

> Of giddy Fortune, but not slide
>   Beyond your service, nor dare venter
>   To wander far from you, the centre.

The very closeness with which Carew has imitated here makes it easy to point to the difference. Donne's figure of the compass, in *A Valediction: forbidding mourning*, is more profound than Carew's adaptation of it. Its neat aptitude may be the first thing that strikes a reader; but he is soon carried beyond mere pleasure in a pretty fancy:

> Thy soule the fixt foot, makes no show
>   To move, but doth, if the'other doe.

> And though it in the center fit,
>   Yet when the other far doth rome,
> It leanes, and hearkens after it,
>   And growes erect, as that comes home.

Such words as "rome," "leanes," "hearkens" gather up emotion into the intellectual image. It seems, as so often in Donne's poems, that one law is at work in all experience. The same flame that lights the intellect warms the heart; mathematics and love obey one principle. The binding of a circle and the union of lovers are equivalent symbols of eternity and perfection:

> Thy firmnes draws my circle just,
>   And makes me end, where I begunne.[1]

Donne's images constantly imply that all phenomena are facets of a single whole. The following extracts illustrate this:

---

[1] The fixed foot of the compass leans towards the other while the circle is being described. When that is completed the out-stretched foot is brought back to the other (the compasses are closed up). While the circle is being described the "firmness" with which the fixed foot is pinned in the centre is what makes the circle "just." My excuse for explaining this figure is that some modern critics have obscured its meaning in their search for ambiguities.

But since my soule, whose child love is,
Takes limmes of flesh, and else could nothing doe,
    More subtile then the parent is,
Love must not be, but take a body too.
                                        Aire and Angels

But as all severall soules containe
    Mixture of things, they know not what,
Love, these mixed soules, doth mixe againe,
    And makes both one, each this and that.
A single violet transplant,
    The strength, the colour, and the size,
(All which before was poore and scant,)
    Redoubles still, and multiplies.
When love, with one another so
    Interinanimates two soules,
That abler soule, which thence doth flow,
    Defects of lonelinesse controules.   *The Extasie*

If, as in water stir'd more circles bee
Produc'd by one, love such additions take,
Those like so many spheares, but one heaven make,
For, they are all concentrique unto thee.
                                        Loves growth.

All poetic images derive from a perception of relation, but
not all lay such stress on an underlying principle of
unity. Donne insists on it. His is the religious temperament, in that he cannot content himself with the tran-
sient and the manifold.

                        On a huge hill,
Cragged, and steep, Truth stands, and hee that will
Reach her, about must, and about must goe;
And what the hills suddennes resists, winne so;[2]

The immediate sense of God was not for him. Vaughan,
Blake, Francis Thompson, were seers or mystics in a sense

2 *Satyre* III.

in which Donne never was. But he shared their desire. Human love was not enough.

> Here the admyring her my mind did whett
> To seeke thee God;[3]

It was not by accident that Donne turned at last to religious poetry and to the pulpit. His direction was manifest in the nature of his images. The poets who best understood their intention were religious poets.

> Let no pious ear be offended [writes Dr. Johnson], if I advance, in opposition to many authorities, that poetical devotion cannot often please. The doctrines of Religion may indeed be defended in a didactick poem, and he who has the happy power of arguing in verse, will not lose it because his subject is sacred. A poet may describe the beauty and grandeur of Nature, the flowers of the Spring, and the harvests of Autumn, the vicissitudes of the Tide, and the revolutions of the Sky, and praise the Maker for his works in lines which no reader shall lay aside. The subject of the disputation is not piety but the motives to piety; that of the description is not God, but the works of God.
>
> Contemplative piety, or the intercourse between God and the human soul, cannot be poetical. Man admitted to implore the mercy of his Creator, and plead the merits of his Redeemer, is already in a higher state than poetry can confer.[4]

Devotional poetry is exposed to attack both from believers like Dr. Johnson and from the sceptical. Johnson rejects it because he assumes that it can add nothing to religious experience; "religion must be shewn as it is; suppression and addition equally corrupt it; and such as it is, it is already known."[5] Meanwhile, the unbelieving reader is

[3] *Holy Sonnet* XVII.
[4] *Life of Waller.*
[5] Ibid.

baffled by the strangeness of what is offered him in devotional poetry. If religious experience means nothing to him, how can he enjoy poetry which is the expression of it? At first sight the complaints seem opposite to one another. For one the subject is too familiar, for the other it is too remote. But both spring from the same misconception. Both assign the wrong kind of importance to the subject of a poem. Poetry is not about things in the same sense in which a prose treatise is about something. A poem expresses, not the thing itself, but the poet's feeling of it. One poet is moved by religious experience, another by human love, another by the song of a bird or the sight of a flower, yet another by a political idea. It does not matter to the reader whether he himself could have been affected by that thing, but only whether the poem affects him. Reading poetry resembles falling in love in the sense in which one "falls in love" whenever one is wholly delighted with another person—a thing that can happen frequently. The intellectual outlook of the object of love, like the belief of the poet, may have no attractions, it may even have been a lifelong antipathy; but when it is associated with a personality that, through some unanalysable quality, stirs the senses and moves the passions, suddenly it is understood, not necessarily nor probably accepted, but felt. Personal charm in the beloved is the equivalent of music and imagery in poetry. In *The Rambler,* no. 86, Johnson talks of the poet's power of "joining musick with reason, and of acting at once upon the senses and the passions," in his *Life of Milton* he speaks of poetry "calling imagination to the help of reason." The excitement experienced by readers of poetry may be due to this sudden binding together of the whole man. The immediate result of such an experience is heightened consciousness. In the state of mind induced by falling in love, or reading a poem, moribund faculties and sympathies are quickened.

Dr. Johnson recognized that a poem should not leave
the reader as it found him. That is the gravamen of his
charge against devotional poetry, for he nowhere envis-
ages an irreligious reader. "Watts' devotional poetry is,
like that of others, unsatisfactory, the paucity of its
topicks enforces perpetual repetition," or of Fenton's
Odes he writes: "As the sentiments are pious they cannot
easily be new, for what can be added to topicks on which
successive ages have been employed?" If the answer be
"nothing," his objection to religious poetry is valid; but it
applies equally to love poetry. The "topicks" presented
by the Christian faith are limited, but so are the "topicks"
suggested by human love. Successive ages have been employed about both. Yet out of these time-worn experiences, poets are continually creating something new.
Even in our own time fresh treasure has been dug from
this mine; this for instance:

The Folly of Being Comforted.

One that is ever kind said yesterday:
"Your well-belovèd's hair has threads of grey,
And little shadows come about her eyes;
Time can but make it easier to be wise
Though now it seems impossible, and so
All that you need is patience."

           Heart cries, "No,
I have not a crumb of comfort, not a grain.
Time can but make her beauty over again:
Because of that great nobleness of hers
The fire that stirs about her, when she stirs,
Burns but more clearly. O she had not these ways
When all the wild summer was in her gaze."

O heart! O heart! if she'd but turn her head,
You'd know the folly of being comforted.[6]

[6] W. B. Yeats.

The distinction is not in the theme, other poets have written about a loved woman growing old. A wistful little poem of Hardy's will serve for comparison:

Wives in the Sere.

Never a careworn wife but shows,
  If a joy suffuse her,
Something beautiful to those
  Patient to peruse her,
Some one charm the world unknows
  Precious to a muser,
Haply what, ere years were foes,
  Moved her mate to choose her.

But, be it a hint of rose
  That an instant hues her,
Or some early light or pose
  Wherewith thought renews her—
Seen by him at full, ere woes
  Practised to abuse her—
Sparely comes it, swiftly goes,
  Time again subdues her.

It is no more than the subject of the two poems that is similar. In its development Yeats combines the loss with the gain; there is no comfort for what is lost; there is no need for comfort, because of what is gained. Hardy lays stress, characteristically, on the cruelty of time and on human tenderness. Even this single aspect of the experience of love, the ageing of the beloved, can be felt and expressed in countless ways. Donne expressed it in *Elegie* IX. *The Autumnal.*

The love of God takes as many different forms, and gives rise to as many different states of mind, as the love of woman. The same beliefs or circumstances produce unendingly varying effects. The fear that poets inspired by Christian beliefs will merely repeat what is already known to the Christian reader need not be seriously

entertained, though it may be replaced by the fear, valid
for all kinds of poetry, that the reader will take nothing
from the poem but what he brought to it.

A more debatable point in our day is, whether there
will be any common ground between the religious poet
and a reader who has no share in Christian beliefs. The
possibility of communication between poet and reader
depends upon there being something in common between them. Fortunately for poetry human needs and
impulses are recurrent, though the directions in which
satisfaction is sought are very varied. The state of mind
in such a poem as Francis Thompson's *The Hound of
Heaven* is readily conveyed to an unbeliever, although it
may have no exact parallel in his experience. The poem
itself, with its abundant imagery and insistent rhythm,
can communicate it:

> I fled Him, down the nights and down the days;
> I fled Him, down the arches of the years;
> I fled Him, down the labyrinthine ways
>   Of my own mind; and in the mist of tears
> I hid from Him, and under running laughter.
>   Up vistaed hopes I sped;
>   And shot, precipitated,
> Adown Titanic glooms of chasmèd fears,
>   From those strong Feet that followed, followed after.
>   But with unhurrying chase,
>   And unperturbèd pace,
> Deliberate speed, majestic instancy,
>   They beat—and a Voice beat
>   More instant than the Feet—
> "All things betray thee, who betrayest Me."

The impulse to escape from the unknown, and the longing to be at one with it, the hurry of thought to avoid
contemplation, the fear of paying too great a price for
what is most desired:

> (For, though I knew His love Who followèd,
>   Yet was I sore adread
> Lest, having Him, I must have nought beside.)

these conflicting impulses are sufficiently common to be intelligible in the guise in which Francis Thompson's faith clothes them. The poem, like Herbert's *Affliction*, is a biography of the human spirit, its adventures may be strange, but the adventurer is familiar. This is likely to be always the case. Poets are rare, but this does not mean that they are different in kind from their readers, they are different in their degree of awareness, their power of co-ordinating experiences, and, chiefly of course, in the nature and degree of their command of words. For a reader of devotional poetry, as of any other kind, the most important qualification is responsiveness to the language and rhythms of poetry. He need not share the poet's beliefs, he may even be more responsive, because more flexible and unreserved, less tempted to foist his own experience on to the poem, if he does not: but he must be susceptible to the poet's power to recreate experience.

Suppose a reader, sensitive to poetry, but repelled by or indifferent to the doctrine of the resurrection of the body, reads Gerard Manley Hopkins' poem, *The Caged Skylark*.

As a dare-gale skylark scanted in a dull cage
   Man's mounting spirit in his bone-house, mean
      house, dwells—
   That bird beyond the remembering his free fells;
This in drudgery, day-labouring-out life's age.

Though aloft on turf or perch or poor low stage,
   Both sing sometimes the sweetest, sweetest spells,
   Yet both droop deadly sómetimes in their cells
Or wring their barriers in bursts of fear or rage.

Not that the sweet-fowl, song-fowl, needs no rest—
Why, hear him, hear him babble and drop down to his
                                    nest,
    But his own nest, wild nest, no prison.
Man's spirit will be flesh-bound when found at best,
But uncumbered: meadow-down is not distressed
    For a rainbow footing it nor he for his bónes rísen.

The poem does not convert such a reader to the doctrine
implied, in the sense in which a theological treatise
might conceivably do so. And yet in some sense the
thought and feeling in the poem are transferred to him.
There is again something in common between poet and
reader to begin with. There can be few who have not felt
the body to be both prison and home, both encumbrance
and delight, both an insufferable limitation and a centre
of rest and refreshment. Such a background of common
experience is all that is needed. The poem does the rest.
Hopkins more even than most poets repays close attention to his verbal pattern. His words are like pieces
in a mosaic, he composes with these fragments. This particular poem is built up in a series of contrasts, the harsh
thuds of the prison motif "scanted in a dull cage"; "in
his bone-house, mean house, dwells—"; "This in drudgery, day-labouring-out life's age"; "Or wring their barriers in bursts of fear or rage"; contrasted with the open,
liquid sound of the free-flight motif: "Man's mounting
spirit"; "remembering his free fells"; "Both sing some-
tímes the sweetest, sweetest spells"; "Why, hear him,
hear him babble and drop down to his nest"; "meadow-
down is not distressed For a rainbow footing it nor he for
his bónes rísen." Finally the reader possesses, not Hopkins' belief, but his feeling of what it would be like to
meet the body again in its resurrected state. Acquaintance with the doctrine concerning the resurrection of the

body is necessary for the poem to be understood, particulary the line which is nearest to prose statement:

> Man's spirit will be flesh-bound when found at best,
> But uncumbered:

but most poetry requires some familiarity with the tradition from which it springs. English poetry, secular or sacred, has its roots in European culture, with its inheritance of Greek, Latin, Hebrew and Christian literatures, the ideas they embody and the gods they celebrate. Given two readers of equal sensibility the more widely read has always an advantage.

Dr. Johnson raised one more objection to devotional poetry which suggests other issues than the familiarity or strangeness of religious experience. "The ideas of Christian Theology are," he writes, "too simple for eloquence, too sacred for fiction, and too majestic for ornament; to recommend them by tropes and figures, is to magnify by a concave mirror the sidereal hemisphere." [7] This assertion is based upon two assumptions, one concerning the means and the other the ends of poetry. In the first place it assumes that poetry is necessarily eloquence; that it achieves its effects by heightening or, as Johnson puts it, "by tropes and figures" which "magnify." He rarely talks nonsense and here, as almost always with him, an important truth is embodied in the questionable verdict. Certain human experiences are beyond eloquence; they can only be expressed with the utmost simplicity. There comes a moment in great tragedy when grandeur of diction, violence of imagery, magnificence of verse can do no more. They give place to unadorned statement:

[7] *Life of Waller.*

> Do not laugh at me;
> For, as I am a man, I think this lady
> To be my child Cordelia.

The ecstasy of religious experience, like the height of tragedy, is beyond the reach of oratory. Verbal elaboration can but travesty such moments; poets use other means. Even Milton, most magniloquent of poets, can lay aside his singing robes, for example, in the closing lines of the sonnet *On his deceased wife*:

> Her face was veiled; yet to my fancied sight
> Love, sweetness, goodness, in her person shined
> So clear as in no face with more delight.
>   But oh! as to embrace me she inclined,
>   I waked, she fled, and day brought back my night.

He uses no eloquence to bewail his blindness. The bare statements "her face was veiled," "and day brought back my night," are enough. Again, no attempt at description could achieve the effect of Vaughan's

> I saw Eternity the other night;[8]

no elaborate words could convey the serene joy of Blake's simple statement:

> The moon like a flower
> In heaven's high bower,
> With silent delight
> Sits and smiles on the night.[9]

The pinnacle of joy or of sorrow can only be treated in poetry when the poet denies himself his ordinary aids. All the verbal tricks that enhance or inflate a theme are set aside, economy of statement is more moving:

---

[8] *The World.*
[9] *Songs of Innocence, Night.*

There a very little girth
Can hold round what once the earth
Seemed to narrow to contain.[1]

Dr. Johnson is right in discerning that some human experiences (and for him religious experience is the type of these) will bear no elaboration. He may have been insensitive to the undertones of poetry, as he was to those of prose (witness his criticisms of Swift). But this is not all. His stricture implies, not only that poetry has no means with which to deal with such experience; but also that it is unworthy of the office. He has in mind a clear conception of what religion is and of what poetry is, and he sets the one beyond the reach of the other. The difficulty here is that the modern commentator cannot meet Dr. Johnson on his own ground. The words poetry and religion comprehend so many kinds of experience, that they no longer seem susceptible of definition, indeed Johnson himself admitted that "to circumscribe poetry by a definition" could "only show the narrowness of the definer."[2] How then is it to be compared with that other elusive experience, religion? Only, probably, by considering, not what either is in itself, but what effects they produce in those who experience them. Poetry and religion each exert power over those who are sensitive to them. There may be fields in which religion operates and poetry does not, as there may be areas of the mind affected by poetry and untouched by faith. But over certain areas both operate. Either can quicken sensibility; either can impose an order upon scattered thoughts and feelings. From one point of view love, or religion, or the beauty of nature can be thought of as materials for poetry, but from another, from that which considers their

[1] Christina Rossetti, *The Bourne.*
[2] *Life of Pope.*

effects, they can be thought of as commensurable with
it. The poet's power over the subtle and complex meanings of words suggests the possibility of perfection, just
as the beloved does to the lover or religion to the be-
liever:

> So in a voice, so in a shapelesse flame
> Angels affect us oft, and worshipped be.[3]

[3] *Aire and Angels.*

THE
Poetry
of
JOHN DONNE

INCONSTANCY

Womans constancy.

Now thou hast lov'd me one whole day,
To morrow when thou leav'st, what wilt thou say?
Wilt thou then Antedate some new made vow?
   Or say that now
We are not just those persons, which we were?
Or, that oathes made in reverentiall feare
Of Love, and his wrath, any may forsweare?
Or, as true deaths, true maryages untie,
So lovers contracts, images of those,
Binde but till sleep, deaths image, them unloose?
   Or, your owne end to Justifie,
For having purpos'd change, and falsehood; you
Can have no way but falsehood to be true?
Vaine lunatique, against these scapes I could
   Dispute, and conquer, if I would,
   Which I abstaine to doe,
For by to morrow, I may thinke so too.

Song.

Goe, and catche a falling starre,
Get with child a mandrake roote,
Tell me, where all past yeares are,
 Or who cleft the Divels foot,
Teach me to heare Mermaides singing,
 Or to keep off envies stinging,
   And finde
   What winde
Serves to advance an honest minde.

If thou beest borne to strange sights,
    Things invisible to see,
Ride ten thousand daies and nights,
    Till age snow white haires on thee,
Thou, when thou retorn'st, will tell mee
All strange wonders that befell thee,
            And sweare
            No where
Lives a woman true, and faire.

If thou findst one, let mee know,
    Such a Pilgrimage were sweet;
Yet doe not, I would not goe,
    Though at next doore wee might meet,
Though shee were true, when you met her,
And last, till you write your letter,
            Yet shee
            Will bee
False, ere I come, to two, or three.

The Indifferent.

I CAN love both faire and browne,
Her whom abundance melts, and her whom want betraies,
Her who loves lonenesse best, and her who maskes and
    plaies,
Her whom the country form'd, and whom the town,
Her who beleeves, and her who tries,
Her who still weepes with spungie eyes,
And her who is dry corke, and never cries;
I can love her, and her, and you and you,
I can love any, so she be not true.

Will no other vice content you?
Will it not serve your turn to do, as did your mothers?
Or have you all old vices spent, and now would finde out
    others?

Or doth a feare, that men are true, torment you?
Oh we are not, be not you so,
Let mee, and doe you, twenty know.
Rob mee, but binde me not, and let me goe.
Must I, who came to travaile thorow you,
Grow your fixt subject, because you are true?
Venus heard me sigh this song,
And by Loves sweetest Part, Variety, she swore,
She heard not this till now; and that it should be so no more.
She went, examin'd, and return'd ere long,
And said, alas, Some two or three
Poore Heretiques in love there bee,
Which thinke to stablish dangerous constancie.
But I have told them, since you will be true,
You shall be true to them, who'are false to you.

The Blossome.

LITTLE think'st thou, poore flower,
   Whom I have watch'd sixe or seaven dayes,
And seene thy birth, and seene what every houre
Gave to thy growth, thee to this height to raise,
And now dost laugh and triumph on this bough,
        Little think'st thou
That it will freeze anon, and that I shall
To morrow finde thee falne, or not at all.

   Little think'st thou poore heart
   That labour'st yet to nestle thee,
And think'st by hovering here to get a part
In a forbidden or forbidding tree,
And hop'st her stiffenesse by long siege to bow:
        Little think'st thou,
That thou to morrow, ere that Sunne doth wake,
Must with this Sunne, and mee a journey take.

But thou which lov'st to bee
   Subtile to plague thy selfe, wilt say,
Alas, if you must goe, what's that to mee?
Here lyes my business, and here I will stay:
You goe to friends, whose love and meanes present
           Various content
To your eyes, eares, and tongue, and every part.
If then your body goe, what need you a heart?

   Well then, stay here; but know,
   When thou hast stayd and done thy most;
A naked thinking heart, that makes no show,
Is to a woman, but a kinde of Ghost;
How shall she know my heart; or having none,
           Know thee for one?
Practise may make her know some other part,
But take my word, shee doth not know a Heart.

   Meet mee at London, then,
   Twenty dayes hence, and thou shalt see
Mee fresher, and more fat, by being with men,
Then if I had staid still with her and thee.
For Gods sake, if you can, be you so too:
           I would give you
There, to another friend, whom wee shall finde
As glad to have my body, as my minde.

LOVE SCORNED

Loves Alchymie.

Some that have deeper digg'd loves Myne then I,
Say, where his centrique happinesse doth lie:
    I have lov'd, and got, and told,
But should I love, get, tell, till I were old,
I should not finde that hidden mysterie;
    Oh, 'tis imposture all:
And as no chymique yet th'Elixar got,
    But glorifies his pregnant pot,
    If by the way to him befall
Some odoriferous thing, or medicinall,
    So, lovers dreame a rich and long delight,
    But get a winter-seeming summers night.

Our ease, our thrift, our honor, and our day,
Shall we, for this vaine Bubles shadow pay?
    Ends love in this, that my man,
Can be as happy'as I can; If he can
Endure the short scorne of a Bridegroomes play?
    That loving wretch that sweares,
'Tis not the bodies marry, but the mindes,
    Which he in her Angelique findes,
    Would sweare as justly, that he heares,
In that dayes rude hoarse minstralsey, the spheares.
    Hope not for minde in women; at their best
    Sweetnesse and wit, they'are but *Mummy*, possest.

Loves Usury.

For every houre that thou wilt spare mee now,
        I will allow,
Usurious God of Love, twenty to thee,

When with my browne, my gray haires equall bee;
Till then, Love, let my body raigne, and let
Mee travell, sojourne, snatch, plot, have, forget,
Resume my last yeares relict: thinke that yet
      We'had never met.

Let mee thinke any rivalls letter mine,
      And at next nine
Keepe midnights promise; mistake by the way
The maid, and tell the Lady of that delay;
Onely let mee love none, no, not the sport;
From country grasse, to comfitures of Court,
Or cities quelque choses, let report
      My minde transport.

This bargaine's good; if when I'am old, I bee
      Inflam'd by thee,
If thine owne honour, or my shame, or paine,
Thou covet most, at that age thou shalt gaine.
Doe thy will then, then subject and degree,
And fruit of love, Love I submit to thee,
Spare mee till then, I'll beare it, though she bee
      One that loves mee.

LOVE'S DELIGHT

The Sunne Rising.

BUSIE old foole, unruly Sunne,
　　Why dost thou thus,
Through windowes, and through curtaines call on us?
Must to thy motions lovers seasons run?
　　　Sawcy pedantique wretch, goe chide
　　　Late schoole boyes, and sowre prentices,
　　Goe tell Court-huntsmen, that the King will ride,
　　Call countrey ants to harvest offices;
Love, all alike, no season knowes, nor clyme,
Nor houres, dayes, moneths, which are the rags of time.

　　　Thy beames, so reverend, and strong
　　　Why shouldst thou thinke?
I could eclipse and cloud them with a winke,
But that I would not lose her sight so long:
　　　If her eyes have not blinded thine,
　　　Looke, and to morrow late, tell mee,
　　Whether both the'India's of spice and Myne
　　Be where thou leftst them, or lie here with mee.
Aske for those Kings whom thou saw'st yesterday,
And thou shalt heare, All here in one bed lay.

　　　She'is all States, and all Princes, I,
　　　Nothing else is.
Princes doe but play us; compar'd to this,
All honor's mimique; All wealth alchimie.
　　　Thou sunne art halfe as happy'as wee,
　　　In that the world's contracted thus;
　　Thine age askes ease, and since thy duties bee
　　To warme the world, that's done in warming us.
Shine here to us, and thou art every where;
This bed thy center is, these walls, thy spheare.

Breake of day.

'Tis true, 'tis day; what though it be?
O wilt thou therefore rise from me?
Why should we rise, because 'tis light?
Did we lie downe, because 'twas night?
Love which in spight of darknesse brought us hether,
Should in despight of light keepe us together.

Light hath no tongue, but is all eye;
If it could speake as well as spie,
This were the worst, that it could say,
That being well, I faine would stay,
And that I lov'd my heart and honor so,
That I would not from him, that had them, goe.

Must businesse thee from hence remove?
Oh, that's the worst disease of love,
The poore, the foule, the false, love can
Admit, but not the busied man.
He which hath businesse, and makes love, doth doe
Such wrong, as when a maryed man doth wooe.

The Dreame.

Deare love, for nothing lesse then thee
Would I have broke this happy dreame,
    It was a theame
For reason, much too strong for phantasie,
Therefore thou wakd'st me wisely; yet
My Dreame thou brok'st not, but continued'st it,
Thou art so truth, that thoughts of thee suffice,
To make dreames truths; and fables histories;
Enter these armes, for since thou thoughtst it best,
Not to dreame all my dreame, let's act the rest.

As lightning, or a Tapers light,
Thine eyes, and not thy noise wak'd mee;
    Yet I thought thee
(For thou lovest truth) an Angell, at first sight,
But when I saw thou sawest my heart,
And knew'st my thoughts, beyond an Angels art,
When thou knew'st what I dreamt, when thou knew'st when
Excesse of joy would wake me, and cam'st then,
I must confesse, it could not chuse but bee
Prophane, to thinke thee any thing but thee.

Comming and staying show'd thee, thee,
But rising makes me doubt, that now,
    Thou art not thou.
That love is weake, where feare's as strong as hee;
'Tis not all spirit, pure, and brave,
If mixture it of *Feare, Shame, Honor,* have.
Perchance as torches which must ready bee,
Men light and put out, so thou deal'st with mee,
Thou cam'st to kindle, goest to come; Then I
Will dreame that hope againe, but else would die.

LOVE UNFULFILLED

Twicknam garden.

BLASTED with sighs, and surrounded with teares,
    Hither I come to seeke the spring,
    And at mine eyes, and at mine eares,
Receive such balmes, as else cure every thing;
    But O, selfe traytor, I do bring
The spider love, which transubstantiates all,
    And can convert Manna to gall,
And that this place may thoroughly be thought
    True Paradise, I have the serpent brought.

'Twere wholsomer for mee, that winter did
    Benight the glory of this place,
    And that a grave frost did forbid
These trees to laugh, and mocke mee to my face;
    But that I may not this disgrace
Indure, nor yet leave loving, Love let mee
    Some senslesse peece of this place bee;
Make me a mandrake, so I may groane here,
    Or a stone fountaine weeping out my yeare.

Hither with christall vyals, lovers come,
    And take my teares, which are loves wine,
    And try your mistresse Teares at home,
For all are false, that tast not just like mine;
    Alas, hearts do not in eyes shine,
Nor can you more judge womans thoughts by teares,
    Then by her shadow, what she weares.
O perverse sexe, where none is true but shee,
    Who's therefore true, because her truth kills mee.

Loves Deitie.

I LONG to talke with some old lovers ghost,
   Who dyed before the god of Love was borne:
I cannot thinke that hee, who then lov'd most,
   Sunke so low, as to love one which did scorne.
But since this god produc'd a destinie,
And that vice-nature, custome, lets it be;
   I must love her, that loves not mee.

Sure, they which make him god, meant not so much,
   Nor he, in his young godhead practis'd it;
But when an even flame two hearts did touch,
   His office was indulgently to fit
Actives to passives. Correspondencie
Only his subject was; It cannot bee
   Love, till I love her, that loves mee.

But every moderne god will now extend
   His vast prerogative, as far as Jove.
To rage, to lust, to write to, to commend,
   All is the purlewe of the God of Love.
Oh were wee wak'ned by this Tyrannie
To ungod this child againe, it could not bee
   I should love her, who loves not mee.

Rebell and Atheist too, why murmure I,
   As though I felt the worst that love could doe?
Love might make me leave loving, or might trie
   A deeper plague, to make her love mee too,
Which, since she loves before, I'am loth to see;
Falshood is worse then hate; and that must bee,
   If shee whom I love, should love mee.

The Funerall.

WHO ever comes to shroud me, do not harme
    Nor question much
That subtile wreath of haire, which crowns my arme;
The mystery, the signe you must not touch,
    For'tis my outward Soule,
Viceroy to that, which then to heaven being gone,
    Will leave this to controule,
And keepe these limbes, her Provinces, from dissolution.

For if the sinewie thread my braine lets fall
    Through every part,
Can tye those parts, and make mee one of all;
These haires which upward grew, and strength and art
    Have from a better braine,
Can better do'it; Except she meant that I
    By this should know my pain,
As prisoners then are manacled, when they'are condemn'd
        to die.

What ere shee meant by'it, bury it with me,
    For since I am
Loves martyr, it might breed idolatrie,
If into others hands these Reliques came;
    As'twas humility
To afford to it all that a Soule can doe,
    So, 'tis some bravery,
That since you would save none of mee, I bury some of you.

LOVE FULFILLED

The Canonization.

For Godsake hold your tongue, and let me love,
  Or chide my palsie, or my gout,
My five gray haires, or ruin'd fortune flout,
    With wealth your state, your minde with Arts improve,
      Take you a course, get you a place,
      Observe his honour, or his grace,
Or the Kings reall, or his stamped face
    Contemplate, what you will, approve,
    So you will let me love.

Alas, alas, who's injur'd by my love?
  What merchants ships have my sighs drown'd?
Who saies my teares have overflow'd his ground?
    When did my colds a forward spring remove?
      When did the heats which my veines fill
      Adde one more to the plaguie Bill?
Soldiers finde warres, and Lawyers finde out still
    Litigious men, which quarrels move,
    Though she and I do love.

Call us what you will, wee are made such by love;
  Call her one, mee another flye,
We'are Tapers too, and at our owne cost die,
    And wee in us finde the'Eagle and the Dove.
      The Phœnix ridle hath more wit
      By us, we two being one, are it.
So to one neutrall thing both sexes fit,
    Wee dye and rise the same, and prove
    Mysterious by this love.

Wee can dye by it, if not live by love,
  And if unfit for tombes and hearse

Our legend bee, it will be fit for verse;
   And if no peece of Chronicle wee prove,
      We'll build in sonnets pretty roomes;
      As well a well wrought urne becomes
The greatest ashes, as halfe-acre tombes,
   And by these hymnes, all shall approve
   Us *Canoniz'd* for Love:

And thus invoke us; You whom reverend love
   Made one anothers hermitage;
You, to whom love was peace, that now is rage;
      Who did the whole worlds soule contract, and drove
      Into the glasses of your eyes
      (So made such mirrors, and such spies,
That they did all to you epitomize,)
   Countries, Townes, Courts: Beg from above
   A patterne of your love!

The good-morrow.

I WONDER by my troth, what thou, and I
Did, till we lov'd? were we not wean'd till then?
But suck'd on countrey pleasures, childishly?
Or snorted we in the seaven sleepers den?
T'was so; but this, all pleasures fancies bee.
If ever any beauty I did see,
Which I desir'd, and got, t'was but a dreame of thee.

And now good morrow to our waking soules,
Which watch not one another out of feare;
For love, all love of other sights controules,
And makes one little roome, an every where.
Let sea-discoverers to new worlds have gone,
Let Maps to other, worlds on worlds have showne,
Let us possesse one world, each hath one, and is one.

My face in thine eye, thine in mine appeares,
And true plaine hearts doe in the faces rest,
Where can we finde two better hemispheares
Without sharpe North, without declining West?

What ever dyes, was not mixt equally;
If our two loves be one, or, thou and I
Love so alike, that none doe slacken, none can die.

The Anniversarie.

ALL Kings, and all their favorites,
    All glory of honors, beauties, wits,
The Sun it selfe, which makes times, as they passe,
Is elder by a yeare, now, then it was
When thou and I first one another saw:
All other things, to their destruction draw,
    Only our love hath no decay;
This, no to morrow hath, nor yesterday,
Running it never runs from us away,
But truly keepes his first, last, everlasting day.

Two graves must hide thine and my coarse,
    If one might, death were no divorce.
Alas, as well as other Princes, wee,
(Who Prince enough in one another bee,)
Must leave at last in death, these eyes, and eares,
Oft fed with true oathes, and with sweet salt teares;
    But soules where nothing dwells but love
(All other thoughts being inmates) then shall prove
This, or a love increased there above,
When bodies to their graves, soules from their graves remove.

And then wee shall be thoroughly blest,
    But wee no more, then all the rest;
Here upon earth, we'are Kings, and none but wee
Can be such Kings, nor of such subjects bee.

Who is so safe as wee? where none can doe
Treason to us, except one of us two.
    True and false feares let us refraine,
Let us love nobly, and live, and adde againe
Yeares and yeares unto yeares, till we attaine
To write threescore: this is the second of our raigne.

Loves infinitenesse.

IF YET I have not all thy love,
Deare, I shall never have it all,
I cannot breath one other sigh, to move,
Nor can intreat one other teare to fall,
And all my treasure, which should purchase thee,
Sighs, teares, and oathes, and letters I have spent.
Yet no more can be due to mee,
Then at the bargaine made was ment,
If then thy gift of love were partiall,
That some to mee, some should to others fall,
    Deare, I shall never have Thee All.

Or if then thou gavest mee all,
All was but All, which thou hadst then;
But if in thy heart, since, there be or shall,
New love created bee, by other men,
Which have their stocks intire, and can in teares,
In sighs, in oathes, and letters outbid mee,
This new love may beget new feares,
For, this love was not vowed by thee.
And yet it was, thy gift being generall,
The ground, thy heart is mine, what ever shall
    Grow there, deare, I should have it all.

Yet I would not have all yet,
Hee that hath all can have no more,
And since my love doth every day admit
New growth, thou shouldst have new rewards in store;

Thou canst not every day give me thy heart,
If thou canst give it, then thou never gavest it:
Loves riddles are, that though thy heart depart,
It stayes at home, and thou with losing savest it:
But wee will have a way more liberall,
Then changing hearts, to joyne them, so wee shall
  Be one, and one anothers All.

Song.

SWEETEST love, I do not goe,
  For wearinesse of thee,
Nor in hope the world can show
  A fitter Love for mee;
    But since that I
Must dye at last, 'tis best,
To use my selfe in jest
  Thus by fain'd deaths to dye;

Yesternight the Sunne went hence,
  And yet is here to day,
He hath no desire nor sense
  Nor halfe so short a way:
    Then feare not mee,
But beleeve that I shall make
Speedier journeyes, since I take
  More wings and spurres then hee.

O how feeble is mans power,
  That if good fortune fall,
Cannot adde another houre,
  Nor a lost houre recall!
    But come bad chance,
And wee joyne to'it our strength,
And wee teach it art and length,
  It selfe o'r us to'advance.

When thou sigh'st, thou sigh'st not winde,
  But sigh'st my soule away,
When thou weep'st, unkindly kinde,
  My lifes blood doth decay.
    It cannot bee
That thou lov'st mee, as thou say'st,
If in thine my life thou waste,
  Thou art the best of mee.

Let not thy divining heart
  Forethinke me any ill,
Destiny may take thy part,
  And may thy feares fulfill;
    But thinke that wee
Are but turn'd aside to sleepe;
They who one another keepe
  Alive, ne'r parted bee.

Loves growth.

I SCARCE beleeve my love to be so pure
  As I had thought it was,
  Because it doth endure
Vicissitude, and season, as the grasse;
Me thinkes I lyed all winter, when I swore,
My love was infinite, if spring make'it more.

But if this medicine, love, which cures all sorrow
With more, not onely bee no quintessence,
But mixt of all stuffes, paining soule, or sense,
And of the Sunne his working vigour borrow,
Love's not so pure, and abstract, as they use
To say, which have no Mistresse but their Muse,
But as all else, being elemented too,
Love sometimes would contemplate, sometimes do.

And yet no greater, but more eminent,
  Love by the spring is growne;
  As, in the firmament,
Starres by the Sunne are not inlarg'd, but showne.
Gentle love deeds, as blossomes on a bough,
From loves awakened root do bud out now.
If, as in water stir'd more circles bee
Produc'd by one, love such additions take,
Those like so many spheares, but one heaven make,
For, they are all concentrique unto thee.
And though each spring doe adde to love new heate,
As princes doe in times of action get
New taxes, and remit them not in peace,
No winter shall abate the springs encrease.

A Valediction: forbidding mourning.

As VIRTUOUS men passe mildly away,
  And whisper to their soules, to goe,
Whilst some of their sad friends doe say,
  The breath goes now, and some say, no:

So let us melt, and make no noise,
  No teare-floods, nor sigh-tempests move,
T'were prophanation of our joyes
  To tell the layetie our love.

Moving of th'earth brings harmes and feares,
  Men reckon what it did and meant,
But trepidation of the spheares,
  Though greater farre, is innocent.

Dull sublunary lovers love
  (Whose soule is sense) cannot admit
Absence, because it doth remove
  Those things which elemented it.

But we by a love, so much refin'd,
  That our selves know not what it is,
Inter-assured of the mind,
  Care lesse, eyes, lips, and hands to misse.

Our two soules therefore, which are one,
  Though I must goe, endure not yet
A breach, but an expansion,
  Like gold to ayery thinnesse beate.

If they be two, they are two so
  As stiffe twin compasses are two,
Thy soule the fixt foot, makes no show
  To move, but doth, if the'other doe.

And though it in the center sit,
  Yet when the other far doth rome,
It leanes, and hearkens after it,
  And growes erect, as that comes home.

Such wilt thou be to mee, who must
  Like th'other foot, obliquely runne;
Thy firmnes makes my circle just,
  And makes me end, where I begunne.

MEDITATIONS ON THE
NATURE OF LOVE

Aire and Angels.

Twice or thrice had I loved thee,
   Before I knew thy face or name;
So in a voice, so in a shapelesse flame,
Angells affect us oft, and worship'd bee;
   Still when, to where thou wert, I came,
Some lovely glorious nothing I did see.
   But since my soule, whose child love is,
Takes limmes of flesh, and else could nothing doe,
   More subtile then the parent is,
Love must not be, but take a body too,
    And therefore what thou wert, and who,
      I bid Love aske, and now
That it assume thy body, I allow,
And fixe it selfe in thy lip, eye, and brow.

Whilst thus to ballast love, I thought,
   And so more steddily to have gone,
With wares which would sinke admiration,
I saw, I had loves pinnace overfraught,
   Ev'ry thy haire for love to worke upon
Is much too much, some fitter must be sought;
   For, nor in nothing, nor in things
Extreme, and scatt'ring bright, can love inhere;
   Then as an Angell, face, and wings
Of aire, not pure as it, yet pure doth weare,
    So thy love may be my loves spheare;
      Just such disparitie
As is twixt Aire and Angells puritie,
'Twixt womens love, and mens will ever bee.

The Extasie.

WHERE, like a pillow on a bed,
    A Pregnant banke swel'd up, to rest
The violets reclining head,
    Sat we two, one anothers best.
Our hands were firmely cimented
    With a fast balme, which thence did spring,
Our eye-beames twisted, and did thred
    Our eyes, upon one double string;
So to'entergraft our hands, as yet
    Was all the meanes to make us one,
And pictures in our eyes to get
    Was all our propagation
As 'twixt two equall Armies, Fate
    Suspends uncertaine victorie,
Our soules, (which to advance their state,
    Were gone out,) hung 'twixt her, and mee.
And whil'st our soules negotiate there,
    Wee like sepulchrall statues lay;
All day, the same our postures were,
    And wee said nothing, all the day.
If any, so by love refin'd,
    That he soules language understood,
And by good love were growen all minde,
    Within convenient distance stood,
He (though he knew not which soule spake,
    Because both meant, both spake the same)
Might thence a new concoction take,
    And part farre purer then he came.
This Extasie doth unperplex
    (We said) and tell us what we love,
Wee see by this, it was not sexe,
    Wee see, we saw not what did move:
But as all severall soules containe
    Mixture of things, they know not what,

Love, these mixt soules, doth mixe againe,
  And makes both one, each this and that.
A single violet transplant,
  The strength, the colour, and the size,
(All which before was poore, and scant,)
  Redoubles still, and multiplies.
When love, with one another so
  Interinanimates two soules,
That abler soule, which thence doth flow,
  Defects of lonelinesse controules.
Wee then, who are this new soule, know,
  Of what we are compos'd, and made,
For, th'Atomies of which we grow,
  Are soules, whom no change can invade.
But O alas, so long, so farre
  Our bodies why doe wee forbeare?
They are ours, though they are not wee, Wee are
  The intelligences, they the spheare.
We owe them thankes, because they thus,
  Did us, to us, at first convay,
Yeelded their forces, sense to us,
  Nor are drosse to us, but allay.
On man heavens influence workes not so,
  But that it first imprints the ayre,
Soe soule into the soule may flow,
  Though it to body first repaire.
As our blood labours to beget
  Spirits, as like soules as it can,
Because such fingers need to knit
  That subtile knot, which makes us man:
So must pure lovers soules descend
  T'affections, and to faculties,
Which sense may reach and apprehend,
  Else a great Prince in prison lies.
To'our bodies turne wee then, that so
  Weake men on love reveal'd may looke;
Loves mysteries in soules doe grow,
  But yet the body is his booke.

And if some lover, such as wee,
   Have heard this dialogue of one,
Let him still marke us, he shall see
   Small change, when we'are to bodies gone.

A nocturnall upon S. Lucies day,
Being the shortest day.

Tis the yeares midnight, and it is the dayes,
Lucies, who scarce seaven houres herself unmaskes,
   The Sunne is spent, and now his flasks
    Send forth light squibs, no constant rayes;
     The worlds whole sap is sunke:
The generall balme th'hydroptique earth hath drunk,
Whither, as to the beds-feet, life is shrunke,
Dead and enterr'd; yet all these seeme to laugh,
Compar'd with me, who am their Epitaph.

Study me then, you who shall lovers bee
At the next world, that is, at the next Spring:
   For I am every dead thing,
    In whom love wrought new Alchimie.
     For his art did expresse
A quintessence even from nothingnesse,
From dull privations, and leane emptinesse:
He ruin'd mee, and I am re-begot
Of absence, darknesse, death; things which are not.

All others, from all things, draw all that's good,
Life, soule, forme, spirit, whence they beeing have;
   I, by loves limbecke, am the grave
    Of all, that's nothing. Oft a flood
     Have wee two wept, and so
Drownd the whole world, us two; oft did we gro
To be to Chaosses, when we did show
Care to ought else; and often absences
Withdrew our soules, and made us carcasses.

But I am by her death, (which word wrongs her)
Of the first nothing, the Elixer grown;
 Were I a man, that I were one,
 I needs must know; I should preferre,
  If I were any beast,
Some ends, some means; Yea plants, yea stones detest,
And love; All, all some properties invest;
If I an ordinary nothing were,
As shadow, a light, and body must be here.

But I am None; nor will my Sunne renew.
You lovers, for whose sake, the lesser Sunne
 At this time to the Goat is runne
 To fetch new lust, and give it you,
  Enjoy your summer all;
Since shee enjoyes her long nights festivall,
Let mee prepare towards her, and let mee call
This houre her Vigill, and her Eve, since this
Both the yeares, and the dayes deep midnight is.

Satyre III.

KINDE pitty chokes my spleene; brave scorn forbids
Those teares to issue which swell my eye-lids;
I must not laugh, nor weepe sinnes, and be wise,
Can railing then cure these worne maladies?
Is not our Mistresse faire Religion,
As worthy of all our Soules devotion,
As vertue was to the first blinded age?
Are not heavens joyes as valiant to asswage
Lusts, as earths honour was to them? Alas,
As wee do them in meanes, shall they surpasse
Us in the end, and shall thy fathers spirit
Meete blinde Philosophers in heaven, whose merit
Of strict life may be imputed faith, and heare
Thee, whom hee taught so easie wayes and neare
To follow, damn'd? O if thou dar'st, feare this;

This feare great courage, and high valour is.
Dar'st thou ayd mutinous Dutch, and dar'st thou lay
Thee in ships woodden Sepulchers, a prey
To leaders rage, to stormes, to shot, to dearth?
Dar'st thou dive seas, and dungeons of the earth?
Hast thou couragious fire to thaw the ice
Of frozen North discoveries? and thrise
Colder then Salamanders, like divine
Children in th'oven, fires of Spaine, and the line,
Whose countries limbecks to our bodies bee,
Canst thou for gaine beare? and must every hee
Which cryes not, Goddesse, to thy Mistresse, draw,
Or eate thy poysonous words? courage of straw!
O desperate coward, wilt thou seeme bold, and
To thy foes and his (who made thee to stand
Sentinell in his worlds garrison) thus yeeld,
And for forbidden warres, leave th'appointed field?
Know thy foes: The foule Devill (whom thou
Strivest to please,) for hate, not love, would allow
Thee faine, his whole Realme to be quit; and as
The worlds all parts wither away and passe,
So the worlds selfe, thy other lov'd foe, is
In her decrepit wayne, and thou loving this
Dost love a withered and worne strumpet; last,
Flesh (it selfes death) and joyes which flesh can taste,
Thou lovest; and thy faire goodly soule, which doth
Give this flesh power to taste joy, thou dost loath.
Seeke true religion. O where? Mirreus
Thinking her unhous'd here, and fled from us,
Seekes her at Rome; there, because hee doth know
That shee was there a thousand yeares agoe,
He loves her ragges so, as wee here obey
The statecloth where the Prince sate yesterday.
Crantz to such brave Loves will not be inthrall'd,
But loves her onely, who at Geneva is call'd
Religion, plaine, simple, sullen, yong,
Contemptuous, yet unhansome; As among
Lecherous humors, there is one that judges

No wenches wholsome, but course country drudges.
Graius stayes still at home here, and because
Some Preachers, vile ambitious bauds, and lawes
Still new like fashions, bid him thinke that shee
Which dwels with us, is onely perfect, hee
Imbraceth her, whom his Godfathers will
Tender to him, being tender, as Wards still
Take such wives as their Guardians offer, or
Pay valewes. Careless Phrygius doth abhorre
All, because all cannot be good, as one
Knowing some women whores, dares marry none.
Graccus loves all as one, and thinkes that so
As women do in divers countries goe
In divers habits, yet are still one kinde,
So doth, so is Religion; and this blind-
nesse too much light breeds; but unmoved thou
Of force must one, and forc'd but one allow;
And the right; aske thy father which is shee,
Let him aske his; though truth and falshood bee
Neare twins, yet truth a little elder is;
Be busie to seeke her, beleeve mee this,
Hee's not of none, nor worst, that seekes the best.
To adore, or scorne an image, or protest,
May all be bad; doubt wisely; in strange way
To stand inquiring right, is not to stray;
To sleepe, or runne wrong, is. On a huge hill,
Cragged, and steep, Truth stands, and hee that will
Reach her, about must, and about must goe;
And what the hills suddennes resists, winne so;

Yet strive so, that before age, deaths twilight,
Thy Soule rest, for none can worke in that night.
To will, implyes delay, therefore now doe:
Hard deeds, the bodies paines; hard knowledge too
The mindes indeavours reach, and mysteries
Are like the Sunne, dazzling, yet plaine to all eyes.
Keepe the truth which thou hast found; men do not stand
In so ill case here, that God hath with his hand

Sign'd Kings blanck-charters to kill whom they hate,
Nor are they Vicars, but hangmen to Fate.
Foole and wretch, wilt thou let thy Soule be tyed
To mans lawes, by which she shall not be tryed
At the last day? Oh, will it then boot thee
To say a Philip, or a Gregory,
A Harry, or a Martin taught thee this?
Is not this excuse for mere contraries,
Equally strong? cannot both sides say so?
That thou mayest rightly obey power, her bounds know;
Those past, her nature, and name is chang'd; to be
Then humble to her is idolatrie.
As streames are, Power is; those blest flowers that dwell
At the rough streames calme head, thrive and do well,
But having left their roots, and themselves given
To the streames tyrannous rage, alas, are driven
Through mills, and rockes, and woods, and at last, almost
Consum'd in going, in the sea are lost:
So perish Soules, which more chuse mens unjust
Power from God claym'd, then God himselfe to trust.

HOLY SONNETS

Holy Sonnet V.

I AM a little world made cunningly
Of Elements, and an Angelike spright,
But black sinne hath betraid to endlesse night
My worlds both parts, and (oh) both parts must die.
You which beyond that heaven which was most high
Have found new sphears, and of new lands can write,
Powre new seas in mine eyes, that so I might
Drowne my world with my weeping earnestly,
Or wash it, if it must be drown'd no more:
But oh it must be burnt! Alas the fire
Of lust and envie have burnt it heretofore,
And made it fouler; Let their flames retire,
And burne me ô Lord, with a fiery zeale
Oh thee and thy house, which doth in eating heale.

Holy Sonnet VII.

AT THE round earths imagin'd corners, blow
Your trumpets, Angells, and arise, arise
From death, you numberlesse infinities
Of soules, and to your scattered bodies goe,
All whom the flood did, and fire shall o'erthrow,
All whom warre, dearth, age, agues, tyrannies,
Despaire, law, chance, hath slaine, and you whose eyes,
Shall behold God, and never tast deaths woe.
But let them sleepe, Lord, and mee mourne a space,
For, if above all these, my sinnes abound,
'Tis late to aske abundance of thy grace,
When wee are there; here on this lowly ground,
Teach mee how to repent; for that's as good
As if thou'hadst seal'd my pardon, with thy blood.

Holy Sonnet XII.

WHY are wee by all creatures waited on?
Why does the prodigall elements supply
Life and food to mee, being more pure than I,
Simple, and further from corruption?
Why brook'st thou, ignorant horse, subjection?
Why dost thou bull, and bore so seelily
Dissemble weaknesse, and by'one mans stroke die,
Whose whole kinde, you might swallow and feed upon?
Weaker I am, woe is mee, and worse then you,
You have not sinn'd, nor need be timorous.
But wonder at a greater wonder, for to us
Created nature doth these things subdue,
But their Creator, whom sin, nor nature tyed,
For us, his Creatures, and his foes, hath dyed.

Holy Sonnet XIV.

BATTER my heart, three person'd God; for you
As yet but knocke, breathe, shine, and seeke to mend;
That I may rise, and stand o'erthrow mee, 'and bend
Your force, to breake, blowe, burn and make me new.
I, like an usurpt towne, to'another due,
Labour to'admit you, but Oh, to no end,
Reason your viceroy in mee, mee should defend,
But is captiv'd, and proves weake or untrue.
Yet dearely'I love you, 'and would be loved faine,
But an betroth'd unto your enemie:
Divorce mee, 'untie, or breake that knot againe,
Take mee to you, imprison mee, for I
Except you'enthrall mee, never shall be free,
Nor ever chast, except you ravish mee.

Holy Sonnet XVII.

SINCE she whom I lov'd hath payd her last debt
To Nature, and to hers, and my good is dead,
And her Soule early into heaven ravished,
Wholly on heavenly things my mind is sett.
Here the admyring her my mind did whett
To seeke thee God; so streames do shew their head;
But though I have found thee, and thou my thirst hast fed,
A holy thirsty dropsy melts mee yett.
But why should I begg more Love, when as thou
Dust wooe my soule for hers; offring all thine:
And dost not only feare least I allow
My Love to Saints and Angels things divine,
But in thy tender jealosy dost doubt
Least the World, Fleshe, yea Devill putt thee out.

Holy Sonnet XIX.

OH, to vex me, contraryes meet in one:
Inconstancy unnaturally hath begott
A constant habit; that when I would not
I change in vowes, and in devotione.
As humorous is my contritione
As my prophane Love, and as soone forgott:
As ridlingly distemper'd, cold and hott,
As praying, as mute; as infinite, as none.
I durst not view heaven yesterday; and to day
In prayers, and flattering speaches I court God:
To morrow I quake with true feare of his rod.
So my devout fitts come and go away
Like a fantastique Ague: save that here
Those are my best dayes, when I shake with feare.

THE
Poetry
of
GEORGE HERBERT

Affliction (1)

WHEN first thou didst entice to thee my heart,
                    I thought the service brave:
So many joyes I write down for my part,
                    Besides what I might have
Out of my stock of naturall delights,
Augmented with thy gracious benefits.

I looked on thy furniture so fine,
                    And made it fine to me:
Thy glorious houshold-stuffe did me entwine,
                    And 'tice me unto thee.
Such starres I counted mine: both heav'n and earth
Payd me my wages in a world of mirth.

What pleasures could I want, whose King I served,
                    Where joyes my fellows were?
Thus argu'd into hopes, my thoughts reserved
                    No place for grief or fear.
Therefore my sudden soul caught at the place,
And made her youth and fiercenesse seek thy face.

At first thou gav'st me milk and sweetnesses;
                    I had my wish and way:
My dayes were straw'd with flow'rs and happinesse;
                    There was no moneth but May.
But with my yeares sorrow did twist and grow,
And made a partie unawares for wo.

My flesh began unto my soul in pain,
                    Sicknesses cleave my bones;
Consuming agues dwell in ev'ry vein,
                    And tune my breath to grones.
Sorrow was all my soul; I scarce beleeved,
Till grief did tell me roundly, that I lived.

When I got health, thou took'st away my life,
                 And more; for my friends die:
My mirth and edge was lost; a blunted knife
                 Was of more use then I.
Thus thinne and lean without a fence or friend,
I was blown through with ev'ry storm and winde.

Whereas my birth and spirit rather took
                 The way that takes the town;
Thou didst betray me to a lingring book,
                 And wrap me in a gown.
I was entangled in the world of strife,
Before I had the power to change my life.

Yet, for I threatened oft the siege to raise,
                 Not simpring all mine age,
Thou often didst with Academick praise
                 Melt and dissolve my rage.
I took thy sweetened pill, till I came where
I could not go away, nor persevere.

Yet lest perchance I should too happie be
                 In my unhappinesse,
Turning my purge to food, thou throwest me
                 Into more sicknesses.
Thus doth thy power crosse-bias me, not making
Thine own gift good, yet me from my wayes taking.

Now I am here, what thou wilt do with me
                 None of my books will show:
I reade, and sigh, and wish I were a tree;
                 For sure then I should grow
To fruit or shade: at least some bird would trust
Her household to me, and I should be just.

Yet, though thou troublest me, I must be meek;
                 In weaknesse must be stout.

Well, I will change the service, and go seek
                    Some other master out.
Ah my deare God! though I am clean forgot,
Let me not love thee, if I love thee not.

Submission.

But that thou art my wisdome, Lord,
        And both mine eyes are thine,
My minde would be extreamly stirr'd
        For missing my designe.

Were it not better to bestow
        Some place and power on me?
Then should thy praises with me grow,
        And share in my degree.

But when I thus dispute and grieve,
        I do resume my sight,
And pilfring what I once did give,
        Disseize thee of thy right.

How know I, if thou shouldst me raise,
        That I should then raise thee?
Perhaps great places and thy praise
        Do not so well agree.

Wherefore unto my gift I stand;
        I will no more advise:
Onely do thou lend me a hand,
        Since thou hast both mine eyes.

The Quip.

The merrie world did on a day
With his train-bands and mates agree

To meet together, where I lay,
And all in sport to geere at me.

First, Beautie crept into a rose,
Which when I pluckt not, Sir, said she,
Tell me, I pray, Whose hands are those?
But thou shalt answer, Lord, for me.

Then Money came, and chinking still,
What tune is this, poore man? said he:
I heard in Musick you had skill.
But thou shalt answer, Lord, for me.

Then came brave Glorie puffing by
In silks that whistled, who but he?
He scarce allow'd me half an eie.
But thou shalt answer, Lord, for me.

Then came quick Wit and Conversation,
And he would needs a comfort be,
And, to be short, make an Oration.
But thou shalt answer, Lord, for me.

Yet when the houre of thy designe
To answer these fine things shall come;
Speak not at large; say, I am thine:
And then they have their answer home.

The Collar.

I STRUCK the board, and cry'd, No more.
            I will abroad.
What? shall I ever sigh and pine?
My lines and life are free; free as the rode,
      Loose as the winde, as large as store.
            Shall I be still in suit?
Have I no harvest but a thorn

To let me bloud, and not restore
What I have lost with cordiall fruit?
    Sure there was wine
Before my sighs did drie it: there was corn
    Before my tears did drown it.
Is the yeare onely lost to me?
    Have I no bayes to crown it?
No flowers, no garlands gay? all blasted?
    All wasted?
Not so, my heart: but there is fruit,
    And thou hast hands.
Recover all thy sigh-blown age
On double pleasures: leave thy cold dispute
Of what is fit, and not. Forsake thy cage,
    Thy rope of sands,
Which pettie thoughts have made, and made to thee
    Good cable, to enforce and draw,
    And be thy law,
While thou didst wink and wouldst not see.
    Away; take heed:
    I will abroad.
Call in thy deaths head there: tie up thy fears.
    He that forbears
    To suit and serve his need,
    Deserves his load.
But as I rav'd and grew more fierce and wilde
    At every word,
Me thoughts I heard one calling, *Child!*
    And I reply'd, *My Lord.*

The Glimpse.

WHITHER away delight?
Thou cam'st but now; wilt thou so soon depart,
    And give me up to night?
For many weeks of lingring pain and smart
But one half houre of comfort to my heart?

Me thinks delight should have
More skill in musick, and keep better time.
Wert thou a winde or wave,
They quickly go and come with lesser crime:
Flowers look about, and die not in their prime.

Thy short abode and stay
Feeds not, but addes to the desire of meat.
Lime begg'd of old, they say,
A neighbour spring to cool his inward heat;
Which by the springs accesse grew much more great.

In hope of thee my heart
Pickt here and there a crumme, and would not die;
But constant to his part,
When as my fears foretold this, did replie,
A slender thread a gentle guest will tie.

Yet if the heart that wept
Must let thee go, return when it doth knock.
Although thy heap be kept
For future times, the droppings of the stock
May oft break forth, and never break the lock.

If I have more to spinne,
The wheel shall go, so that thy stay be short.
Thou knowst how grief and sinne
Disturb the work. O make me not their sport,
Who by thy coming may be made a court!

The Flower.

How fresh, O Lord, how sweet and clean
Are thy returns! ev'n as the flowers in spring;
To which, besides their own demean,
The late-past frosts tributes of pleasure bring.

Grief melts away
Like snow in May,
As if there were no such cold thing.

Who would have thought my shrivel'd heart
Could have recover'd greennesse? It was gone
Quite under ground; as flowers depart
To see their mother-root, when they have blown;
Where they together
All the hard weather,
Dead to the world, keep house unknown.

These are thy wonders, Lord of power,
Killing and quickning, bringing down to hell
And up to heaven in an houre;
Making a chiming of a passing-bell.
We say amisse,
This or that is:
Thy word is all, if we could spell.

O that I once past changing were,
Fast in thy Paradise, where no flower can wither!
Many a spring I shoot up fair,
Offring at heav'n growing and groning thither:
Nor doth my flower
Want a spring-showre,
My sinnes and I joining together.

But while I grow in a straight line,
Still upwards bent, as if heav'n were mine own,
Thy anger comes, and I decline:
What frost to that? what pole is not the zone,
Where all things burn,
When thou dost turn,
And the least frown of thine is shown?

And now in age I bud again,
After so many deaths I live and write;

I once more smell the dew and rain,
And relish versing: O my onely light,
                    It cannot be
                    That I am he
On whom thy tempests fell all night.

These are thy wonders, Lord of love,
To make us see we are but flowers that glide:
    Which when we once can finde and prove,
Thou hast a garden for us, where to bide.
                    Who would be more,
                    Swelling through store,
Forfeit their Paradise by their pride.

Church-lock and key.

I KNOW it is my sinne, which locks thine eares,
                    And bindes thy hands,
Out-crying my requests, drowning my tears;
Or else the chilnesse of my faint demands.

But as cold hands are angrie with the fire,
                    And mend it still;
So I do lay the want of my desire,
Not on my sinnes, or coldnesse, but thy will.

Yet heare, O God, onely for his blouds sake
                    Which pleads for me:
For though sinnes plead too, yet like stones they make
His blouds sweet current much more loud to be.

Frailtie.

LORD, in my silence how do I despise
                    What upon trust
Is styled *honour, riches,* or *fair eyes;*

But is *fair dust!*
I surname them *guilded clay,*
   Deare earth, fine grasse or *hay;*
In all, I think my foot doth ever tread
     Upon their head.

But when I view abroad both Regiments;
     The worlds, and thine:
Thine clad with simplenesse, and sad events;
     The other fine,
Full of glorie and gay weeds,
   Brave language, braver deeds:
That which was dust before, doth quickly rise,
     And prick mine eyes.

O brook not this, lest if what even now
     My foot did tread,
Affront those joyes, wherewith thou didst endow
     And long since wed
My poore soul, ev'n sick of love:
   It may a Babel prove
Commodious to conquer heav'n and thee
     Planted in me.

Deniall.

WHEN my devotions could not pierce
     Thy silent eares;
Then was my heart broken, as was my verse:
     My breast was full of fears
      And disorder:

My bent thoughts, like a brittle bow,
     Did flie asunder:
Each took his way; some would to pleasures go,
     Some to the warres and thunder
      Of alarms.

As good go any where, they say,
                    As to benumme
Both knees and heart, in crying night and day,
                    Come, come, my God, O come,
                              But no hearing.

O that thou shouldst give dust a tongue
                    To crie to thee,
And then not heare it crying! all day long
                    My heart was in my knee,
                              But no hearing.

Therefore my soul lay out of sight,
                    Untun'd, unstrung:
My feeble spirit, unable to look right,
                    Like a nipt blossome, hung
                              Discontented.

O cheer and tune my heartlesse breast,
                    Deferre no time;
That so thy favours granting my request,
                    They and my minde may chime,
                              And mend my ryme.

The Pearl. Matth. 13. 45.

I KNOW the wayes of Learning; both the head
And pipes that feed the presse, and make it runne;
What reason hath from nature borrowed,
Or of it self, like a good huswife, spunne
In laws and policie; what the starres conspire,
What willing nature speaks, what forc'd by fire;
Both th' old discoveries, and the new-found seas,
The stock and surplus, cause and historie:
All these stand open, or I have the keyes:
                    Yet I love thee.

I know the wayes of Honour, what maintains
The quick returns of courtesie and wit:
In vies of favours whether partie gains,
When glorie swells the heart, and moldeth it
To all expressions both of hand and eye,
Which on the world a true-love-knot may tie,
And bear the bundle, wheresoe're it goes:
How many drammes of spirit there must be
To sell my life unto my friends or foes:
           Yet I love thee.

I know the wayes of Pleasure, the sweet strains,
The lullings and the relishes of it;
The propositions of hot bloud and brains;
What mirth and musick mean; what love and wit
Have done these twentie hundred yeares, and more:
I know the projects of unbridled store:
My stuffe is flesh, not brasse; my senses live,
And grumble oft, that they have more in me
Then he that curbs them, being but one to five:
           Yet I love thee.

I know all these, and have them in my hand:
Therefore not sealed, but with open eyes
I flie to thee, and fully understand
Both the main sale, and the commodities;
And at what rate and price I have thy love;
With all the circumstances that may move:
Yet through these labyrinths, not my groveling wit,
But thy silk twist let down from heav'n to me,
Did both conduct and teach me, how by it
           To climbe to thee.

Employment (1).

IF as a flowre doth spread and die,
    Thou wouldst extend me to some good,

Before I were by frosts extremitie
                    Nipt in the bud;

The sweetnesse and the praise were thine;
    But the extension and the room,
Which in thy garland I should fill, were mine
                    At thy great doom.

For as thou dost impart thy grace,
    The greater shall our glorie be.
The measure of our joyes is in this place,
                    The stuffe with thee.

Let me not languish then, and spend
    A life as barren to thy praise,
As is the dust, to which that life doth tend,
                    But with delaies.

All things are busie; onely I
    Neither bring hony with the bees,
Nor flowres to make that, nor the husbandrie
                    To water these.

I am no link of thy great chain,
    But all my companie is a weed.
Lord place me in thy consort; give one strain
                    To my poore reed.

The Temper (1)

How should I praise thee, Lord! how should my rymes
    Gladly engrave thy love in steel,
If what my soul doth feel sometimes,
    My soul might ever feel!

Although there were some fourtie heav'ns, or more,
    Sometimes I peere above them all;

Sometimes I hardly reach a score,
　　Sometimes to hell I fall.

O rack me not to such a vast extent;
　　Those distances belong to thee:
The world's too little for thy tent,
　　A grave too big for me.

Wilt thou meet arms with man, that thou dost stretch
　　A crumme of dust from heav'n to hell?
Will great God measure with a wretch?
　　Shall he thy stature spell?

O let me, when thy roof my soul hath hid,
　　O let me roost and nestle there:
Then of a sinner thou art rid,
　　And I of hope and fear.

Yet take thy way; for sure thy way is best:
　　Stretch or contract me, thy poore debter:
This is but tuning of my breast,
　　To make the musick better.

Whether I flie with angels, fall with dust,
　　Thy hands made both, and I am there:
Thy power and love, my love and trust
　　Make one place ev'ry where.

*　　*　　*

Love

I.

IMMORTALL Love, author of this great frame,
　　Sprung from that beautie which can never fade;
　　How hath man parcel'd out thy glorious name,
And thrown it on that dust which thou hast made,
While mortall love doth all the title gain!

Which siding with invention, they together
Bear all the sway, possessing heart and brain,
(Thy workmanship) and give thee share in neither.
Wit fancies beautie, beautie raiseth wit:
    The world is theirs; they two play out the game,
    Thou standing by: and though thy glorious name
Wrought our deliverance from th' infernall pit,
    Who sings thy praise? onely a skarf or glove
    Doth warm our hands, and make them write of love.

II.

IMMORTALL Heat, O let thy greater flame
    Attract the lesser to it: let those fires,
    Which shall consume the world, first make it tame;
And kindle in our hearts such true desires,
As may consume our lusts, and make thee way.
    Then shall our hearts pant thee; then shall our brain
    All her invention on thine Altar lay,
And there in hymnes send back thy fire again:
Our eies shall see thee, which before saw dust;
    Dust blown by wit, till that they both were blinde:
    Thou shalt recover all thy goods in kinde,
Who wert disseized by usurping lust:
    All knees shall bow to thee; all wits shall rise,
    And praise him who did make and mend our eies.

Dulnesse.

WHY do I languish thus, drooping and dull,
                As if I were all earth?
O give me quicknesse, that I may with mirth
                Praise thee brim-full!

The wanton lover in a curious strain
                Can praise his fairest fair;

And with quaint metaphors her curled hair
        Curl o're again.

Thou art my lovelinesse, my life, my light,
        Beautie alone to me:
Thy bloudy death and undeserv'd, makes thee
        Pure red and white.

When all perfections as but one appeare,
        That those thy form doth show,
The very dust, where thou dost tread and go,
        Makes beauties here.

Where are my lines then? my approaches? views?
        Where are my window-songs?
Lovers are still pretending, & ev'n wrongs
        Sharpen their Muse:

But I am lost in flesh, whose sugred lyes
        Still mock me, and grow bold:
Sure thou didst put a minde there, if I could
        Finde where it lies.

Lord, cleare thy gift, that with a constant wit
        I may but look towards thee:
Look onely; for to *love* thee, who can be,
        What angel fit?

Jordan (1)

WHO sayes that fictions onely and false hair
Become a verse? Is there in truth no beautie?
Is all good structure in a winding stair?
May no lines passe, except they do their dutie
    Not to a true, but painted chair?

Is it no verse, except enchanted groves
And sudden arbours shadow course-spunne lines?
Must purling streams refresh a lovers loves?
Must all be vail'd, while he that reades, divines,
  Catching the sense at two removes?

Shepherds are honest people; let them sing:
Riddle who list, for me, and pull for Prime:
I envie no mans nightingale or spring;
Nor let them punish me with losse of rime,
  Who plainly say, *My God, My King.*

*   *   *

The H. Scriptures.

I.

OH BOOKE! infinite sweetnesse! let my heart
  Suck ev'ry letter, and a hony gain,
  Precious for any grief in any part;
To cleare the breast, to mollifie all pain.
Thou art all health, health thriving till it make
  A full eternitie: thou art a masse
  Of strange delights, where we may wish & take.
Ladies, look here; this is the thankfull glasse,
That mends the lookers eyes: this is the well
  That washes what it shows. Who can indeare
  Thy praise too much? thou art heav'ns Lidger here,
Working against the states of death and hell.
  Thou art joyes handsell: heav'n lies flat in thee,
  Subject to ev'ry mounters bended knee.

II.

Oh that I knew how all thy lights combine,
  And the configurations of their glorie!
  Seeing not onely how each verse doth shine,

But all the constellations of the storie.
This verse marks that, and both do make a motion
    Unto a third, that ten leaves off doth lie:
    Then as dispersed herbs do watch a potion,
These three make up some Christians destinie:
Such are thy secrets, which my life makes good,
    And comments on thee: for in ev'ry thing
    Thy words do finde me out, & parallels bring,
And in another make me understood.

    Starres are poore books, & oftentimes do misse:
    This book of starres lights to eternall blisse.

Grace.

My stock lies dead, and no increase
Doth my dull husbandrie improve:
O let thy graces without cease
          Drop from above!

If still the sunne should hide his face,
Thy house would but a dungeon prove,
Thy works nights captives: O let grace
          Drop from above!

The dew doth ev'ry morning fall;
And shall the dew out-strip thy Dove?
The dew, for which grasse cannot call,
          Drop from above.

Death is still working like a mole,
And digs my grave at each remove:
Let grace work too, and on my soul
          Drop from above.

Sinne is still hammering my heart
Unto a hardnesse, void of love:
Let suppling grace, to crosse his art,
          Drop from above.

O come! for thou dost know the way:
Or if to me thou wilt not move,
Remove me, where I need not say,
       Drop from above!

The Agonie.

PHILOSOPHERS have measur'd mountains,
Fathom'd the depths of seas, of states, and kings,
Walk'd with a staffe to heav'n, and traced fountains:
    But there are two vast, spacious things,
The which to measure it doth more behove:
Yet few there are that sound them; Sinne and Love.

Who would know Sinne, let him repair
Unto Mount Olivet; there shall he see
A man so wrung with pains, that all his hair,
    His skinne, his garments bloudie be.
Sinne is that presse and vice, which forceth pain
To hunt his cruell food through ev'ry vein.

Who knows not Love, let him assay
And taste that juice, which on the crosse a pike
Did set again abroach; then let him say
    If ever he did taste the like.
Love is that liquor sweet and most divine,
Which my God feels as bloud; but I, as wine.

Sepulchre.

O BLESSED bodie! Whither art thou thrown?
No lodging for thee, but a cold hard stone?
So many hearts on earth, and yet not one
       Receive thee?
Sure there is room within our hearts good store;
For they can lodge transgressions by the score:

Thousands of toyes dwell there, yet out of doore
          They leave thee.

But that which shews them large, shews them unfit.
What ever sinne did this pure rock commit,
Which holds thee now? Who hath indited it
          Of murder?
Where our hard hearts have took up stones to brain thee,
And missing this, most falsly did arraigne thee;
Onely these stones in quiet entertain thee,
          And order.

And as of old the Law by heav'nly art
Was writ in stone; so thou, which also art
The letter of the word, find'st no fit heart
          To hold thee.
Yet do we still persist as we began,
And so should perish, but that nothing can,
Though it be cold, hard, foul, from loving man
          Withhold thee.

H. Baptisme (II).

          SINCE, Lord, to thee
     A narrow way and little gate
Is all the passage, on my infancie
     Thou didst lay hold, and antedate
          My faith in me.

          O let me still
     Write thee great God, and me a childe:
Let me be soft and supple to thy will,
     Small to my self, to others milde,
          Behither ill.

          Although by stealth
     My flesh get on, yet let her sister

My soul bid nothing, but preserve her wealth:
      The growth of flesh is but a blister;
        Childhood is health.

Prayer (1).

PRAYER the Churches banquet, Angels age,
Gods breath in man returning to his birth,
    The soul in paraphrase, heart in pilgrimage,
The Christian plummet sounding heav'n and earth;
Engine against th' Almightie, sinners towre,
      Reversed thunder, Christ-side-piercing spear,
    The six-daies world transposing in an houre,
A kinde of tune, which all things heare and fear;
Softnesse, and peace, and joy, and love, and blisse,
      Exalted Manna, gladnesse of the best,
      Heaven in ordinarie, man well drest,
The milkie way, the bird of Paradise,
      Church-bels beyond the starres heard, the souls bloud,
      The land of spices; something understood.

Sinne (11)

O THAT I could a sinne once see!
    We paint the devil foul, yet he
    Hath some good in him, all agree.
Sinne is flat opposite to th' Almighty, seeing
It wants the good of *vertue,* and of *being*.

But God more care of us hath had:
    If apparitions make us sad,
    By sight of sinne we should grow mad.
Yet as in sleep we see foul death, and live:
So devils are our sinnes in perspective.

Ungratefulnesse.

LORD, with what bountie and rare clemencie
      Hast thou redeem'd us from the grave!
        If thou hadst let us runne,
        Gladly had man ador'd the sunne,
        And thought his god most brave;
Where now we shall be better gods then he.

Thou hast but two rare cabinets full of treasure,
      The *Trinitie*, and *Incarnation*:
        Thou hast unlockt them both,
        And made them jewels to betroth
        The work of thy creation
Unto thy self in everlasting pleasure.

The statelier cabinet is the *Trinitie*,
      Whose sparkling light accesse denies:
        Therefore thou dost not show
        This fully to us, till death blow
        The dust into our eyes:
For by that powder thou wilt make us see.

But all thy sweets are packt up in the other;
      Thy mercies thither flock and flow:
        That as the first affrights,
        This may allure us with delights;
        Because this box we know;
For we have all of us just such another.

But man is close, reserv'd, and dark to thee:
      When thou demandest but a heart,
        He cavils instantly.
        In his poore cabinet of bone
        Sinnes have their box apart,
Defrauding thee, who gavest two for one.

Vertue.

SWEET day, so cool, so calm, so bright,
The bridall of the earth and skie:
The dew shall weep thy fall to night;
    For thou must die.

Sweet rose, whose hue angrie and brave
Bids the rash gazer wipe his eye:
Thy root is ever in its grave,
    And thou must die.

Sweet spring, full of sweet dayes and roses,
A box where sweets compacted lie;
My musick shows ye have your closes,
    And all must die.

Onely a sweet and vertuous soul,
Like season'd timber, never gives;
But though the whole world turn to coal,
    Then chiefly lives.

The Pulley.

WHEN God at first made man,
Having a glasse of blessings standing by;
Let us (said he) poure on him all we can:
Let the worlds riches, which dispersed lie,
   Contract into a span.

So strength first made a way;
Then beautie flow'd, then wisdome, honour, pleasure:
When almost all was out, God made a stay,
Perceiving that alone of all his treasure
   Rest in the bottome lay.

For if I should (said he)
Bestow this jewell also on my creature,
He would adore my gifts in stead of me,
And rest in Nature, not the God of Nature:
So both should losers be.

Yet let him keep the rest,
But keep them with repining restlesnesse:
Let him be rich and wearie, that at least,
If goodnesse leade him not, yet wearinesse
May tosse him to my breast.

Death.

DEATH, thou wast once an uncouth hideous thing,
Nothing but bones,
The sad effect of sadder grones:
Thy mouth was open, but thou couldst not sing.

For we consider'd thee as at some six
Or ten yeares hence,
After the losse of life and sense,
Flesh being turn'd to dust, and bones to sticks.

We lookt on this side of thee, shooting short;
Where we did finde
The shells of fledge souls left behinde,
Dry dust, which sheds no tears, but may extort.

But since our Saviours death did put some bloud
Into thy face;
Thou art grown fair and full of grace,
Much in request, much sought for as a good.

For we do now behold thee gay and glad,
As at dooms-day;

When souls shall wear their new aray,
And all thy bones with beautie shall be clad.

Therefore we can go die as sleep, and trust
Half that we have
Unto an honest faithfull grave;
Making our pillows either down, or dust.

THE
Poetry
of
HENRY VAUGHAN

The Match

DEAR friend! whose holy, ever-living lines
Have done much good
To many, and have checkt my blood,
My fierce, wild blood that still heaves, and inclines,
But is still tam'd
By those bright fires which thee inflam'd;
Here I joyn hands, and trust my stubborn heart
Into thy *Deed*,
There from no *Duties* to be freed,
And if hereafter *youth*, or *folly* thwart
And claim their share,
Here I renounce the pois'nous ware.

ii

Accept, dread Lord, the poor Oblation,
It is but poore,
Yet through thy Mercies may be more.
O thou! that canst not wish my souls damnation
Afford me life,
And save me from all inward strife!
Two *Lifes* I hold from thee, my gracious Lord,
Both cost thee deer,
For one, I am thy Tenant here;
The other, the true life, in the next world
And endless is,
O let me still mind *that* in *this!*
To thee therefore my *Thoughts, Words, Actions*
I do resign,
Thy will in all be done, not mine.
Settle my *house,* and shut out all distractions
That may unknit
My heart, and thee planted in it;
Lord *Jesu!* thou didst bow thy blessed head
Upon a tree,

O do as much, now unto me!
O hear, and heal thy servant! Lord, strike dead
All lusts in me,
Who onely wish life to serve thee?
Suffer no more this dust to overflow
And drown my eies,
But seal, or pin them to thy skies.
And let this *grain* which here in tears I sow
Though *dead,* and *sick,*
Through thy *Increase* grow *new,* and *quick.*

The Pursuite.

LORD! what a busie, restles thing
Hast thou made man?
Each day, and houre he is on wing,
Rests not a span;
Then having lost the Sunne, and light
By clouds surpriz'd
He keepes a Commerce in the night
With aire disguis'd;
Hadst thou given to this active dust
A state untir'd,
The lost Sonne had not left the huske
Nor home desir'd;
That was thy secret, and it is
Thy mercy too,
For when all failes to bring to blisse,
Then, this must doe.
Ah! Lord! and what a Purchase will that be
To take us sick, that sound would not take thee?

Mount of Olives.

SWEETE, sacred hill! on whose fair brow
My Saviour sate, shall I allow
Language to love

And Idolize some shade, or grove,
Neglecting thee? such ill-plac'd wit,
Conceit, or call it what you please
  Is the braines fit,
   And meere disease;

2.

Cotswold, and *Coopers* both have met
With learned swaines, and Eccho yet
  Their pipes, and wit;
But thou sleep'st in a deepe neglect
Untouch'd by any; And what need
The sheep bleat thee a silly Lay
   That heard'st both reed
   And sheepward play?

3.

Yet, if Poets mind thee well
They shall find thou art their hill,
  And fountaine too,
Their Lord with thee had most to doe;
He wept once, walkt whole nights on thee,
And from thence (his suff'rings ended,)
   Unto glorie
   Was attended;

4.

Being there, this spacious ball
Is but his narrow footstoole all,
  And what we thinke
Unsearchable, now with one winke
He doth comprise; But in this aire
When he did stay to beare our Ill
   And sinne, this Hill
   Was then his Chaire.

Man.

WEIGHING the stedfastness and state
Of some mean things which here below reside,
Where birds like watchful Clocks the noiseless date
   And Intercourse of times divide,
Where Bees at night get home and hive, and flowrs
      Early, aswel as late,
Rise with the Sun, and set in the same bowrs;

2.

I would (said I) my God would give
The staidness of these things to man! for these
To his divine appointments ever cleave,
   And no new business breaks their peace;
The birds nor sow, nor reap, yet sup and dine,
      The flowres without clothes live,
Yet *Solomon* was never drest so fine.

3.

Man hath stil either toyes, or Care,
He hath no root, nor to one place is ty'd,
But ever restless and Irregular
   About this Earth doth run and ride,
He knows he hath a home, but scarce knows where,
      He sayes it is so far
That he hath quite forgot how to go there.

4.

He knocks at all doors, strays and roams,
Nay hath not so much wit as some stones have
Which in the darkest nights point to their homes,
   By some hid sense their Maker gave;

Man is the shuttle, to whose winding quest
    And passage through these looms
God order'd motion, but ordain'd no rest.

The Retreate.

HAPPY those early dayes! when I
Shin'd in my Angell-infancy.
Before I understood this place
Appointed for my second race,
Or taught my soul to fancy ought
But a white, Celestiall thought,
When yet I had not walkt above
A mile, or two, from my first love,
And looking back (at that short space,)
Could see a glimpse of his bright-face;
When on some *gilded Cloud,* or *flowre*
My gazing soul would dwell an houre,
And in those weaker glories spy
Some shadows of eternity;
Before I taught my tongue to wound
My Conscience with a sinfull sound,
Or had the black art to dispence
A sev'rall sinne to ev'ry sence,
But felt through all this fleshly dresse
Bright *shootes* of everlastingnesse.
    O how I long to travell back
And tread again that ancient track!
That I might once more reach that plaine,
Where first I left my glorious traine,
From whence th' Inlightned spirit sees
That shady City of Palme trees;
But (ah!) my soul with too much stay
Is drunk, and staggers in the way.
Some men a forward motion love,
But I by backward steps would move,
And when this dust falls to the urn
In that state I came return.

Childe-hood.

I CANNOT reach it; and my striving eye
Dazles at it, as at eternity.
    Were now that Chronicle alive,
Those white designs which children drive,
And the thoughts of each harmless hour,
With their content too in my pow'r,
Quickly would I make my path even,
And by meer playing go to Heaven.
      Why should men love
A Wolf, more then a Lamb or Dove?
Or choose hell-fire and brimstone streams
Before bright stars, and Gods own beams?
Who kisseth thorns, will hurt his face,
But flowers do both refresh and grace,
And sweetly living (*fie on men!*)
Are when dead, medicinal then.
If seeing much should make staid eyes,
And long experience should make wise;
Since all that age doth teach, is ill,
Why should I not love childe-hood still?
Why if I see a rock or shelf,
Shall I from thence cast down my self,
Or by complying with the world,
From the same precipice be hurl'd?
Those observations are but foul
Which make me wise to lose my soul.

And yet the *Practice* worldlings call
Business and weighty action all,
Checking the poor childe for his play,
But gravely cast themselves away.

    Dear, harmless age! the short, swift span,
Where weeping virtue parts with man;

Where love without lust dwells, and bends
What way we please, without self-ends.

An age of mysteries! which he
Must live twice, that would Gods face see;
Which *Angels* guard, and with it play,
Angels! which foul men drive away.

How do I study now, and scan
Thee, more then ere I studyed man,
And onely see through a long night
Thy edges, and thy bordering light!
O for thy Center and mid-day!
For sure that is the *narrow way*.

The Evening-watch.
A Dialogue.

FAREWELL! I goe to sleep; but when   *Body.*
The day-star springs, I'le wake agen.
  Goe, sleep in peace; and when thou lyest   *Soul.*
Unnumber'd in thy dust, when all this frame
Is but one dramme, and what thou now descriest
  In sev'rall parts shall want a name,
Then may his peace be with thee, and each dust
Writ in his book, who ne'r betray'd mans trust!
  Amen! but hark, e'r we two stray,   *Body.*
  How many hours do'st think 'till day?
  Ah! go; th'art weak, and sleepie. Heav'n   *Soul.*
Is a plain watch, and without figures winds
All ages up; who drew this Circle even
  He fils it; Dayes, and hours are *Blinds.*
Yet, this take with thee; The last gasp of time
Is thy first breath, and mass *eternall Prime.*

Midnight.

WHEN to my Eyes
(Whilst deep sleep others catches,)
        Thine hoast of spyes
The starres shine in their watches,
        I doe survey
        Each busie Ray,
And how they work, and wind,
        And wish each beame
        My soul doth streame,
With the like ardour shin'd;
        What Emanations,
        Quick vibrations
And bright stirs are there?
        What thin Ejections,
        Cold Affections,
    And slow motions here?

2.

        Thy heav'ns (some say,)
Are a firie-liquid light,
        Which mingling aye
Streames, and flames thus to the sight.
        Come then, my god!
        Shine on this bloud,
And water in one beame,
        And thou shalt see
        Kindled by thee
Both liquors burne, and streame.
        O what bright quicknes,
        Active brightnes,
And celestiall flowes
        Will follow after
        On that water,
Which thy spirit blowes!

Math. Cap. 3. ver. xi.

I indeed baptize you with water unto repentance,
but he that commeth after me, is mightier than I,
whose shooes I am not worthy to beare, he shall bap-
tize you with the holy Ghost, and with fire.

The Dawning.

Ah! what time wilt thou come? when shall that crie
   The *Bridegroome's Coming!* fil the sky?
   Shall it in the Evening run
   When our words and works are done?
   Or wil thy all-surprizing light
     Break at midnight?
When either sleep, or some dark pleasure
Possesseth mad man without measure;
Or shal these early, fragrant hours
   Unlock thy bowres?
And with their blush of light descry
Thy locks crown'd with eternitie;
Indeed, it is the only time
That with thy glory doth best chime,
All now are stirring, ev'ry field
   Ful hymns doth yield,
The whole Creation shakes off night,
And for thy shadow looks the light,
Stars now vanish without number,
Sleepie Planets set, and slumber,
The Pursie Clouds disband, and scatter,
All expect some sudden matter,
Not one beam triumphs, but from far
   That morning-star;

O at what time soever thou
(Unknown to us,) the heavens wilt bow,
And, with thy Angels in the *Van*,
Descend to Judge poor careless man,

Grant, I may not like puddle lie
In a Corrupt securitie,
Where, if a traveller water crave,
He finds it dead, and in a grave;
But as this restless, vocall *Spring*
All day, and night doth run, and sing,
And though here born, yet is acquainted
Elsewhere, and flowing keeps untainted;
So let me all my busie age
In thy free services ingage,
And though (while here) of force I must
Have Commerce sometimes with poor dust,
And in my flesh, though vile, and low,
As this doth in her Channel, flow,
Yet let my Course, my aym, my Love,
And chief acquaintance be above;
So when that day, and hour shal come
In which thy self wil be the Sun,
Thou'lt find me drest and on my way,
Watching the Break of thy great day.

Easter Hymn.

DEATH, and darkness get you packing,
Nothing now to man is lacking,
All your triumphs now are ended,
And what *Adam* marr'd, is mended;
Graves are beds now for the weary,
Death a nap, to wake more merry;
Youth now, full of pious duty,
Seeks in thee for perfect beauty,
The weak, and aged tir'd, with length
Of daies, from thee look for new strength,
And Infants with thy pangs Contest
As pleasant, as if with the brest;

    Then, unto him, who thus hath thrown
Even to Contempt thy kingdome down,

And by his blood did us advance
Unto his own Inheritance,
To him be glory, power, praise,
From this, unto the last of daies.

Unprofitableness.

How rich, O Lord! how fresh thy visits are!
'Twas but Just now my bleak leaves hopeles hung
    Sullyed with dust and mud;
Each snarling blast shot through me, and did share
Their Youth, and beauty, Cold showres nipt, and wrung
    Their spiciness, and bloud;
But since thou didst in one sweet glance survey
Their sad decays, I flourish, and once more
    Breath all perfumes, and spice;
I smell a dew like *Myrrh*, and all the day
Wear in my bosome a full Sun; such store
    Hath one beame from thy Eys.
But, ah, my God; what fruit hast thou of this?
What one poor leaf did ever I yet fall
    To wait upon thy wreath?
Thus thou all day a thankless weed doest dress,
And when th'hast done, a stench, or fog is all
    The odour I bequeath.

Silence, and stealth of dayes!

SILENCE, and stealth of dayes! 'tis now
      Since thou art gone,
Twelve hundred houres, and not a brow
      But Clouds hang on.
As he that in some Caves thick damp
      Lockt from the light,
Fixeth a solitary lamp,
      To brave the night

And walking from his Sun, when past
                    That glim'ring Ray
Cuts through the heavy mists in haste
                    Back to his day,
So o'r fled minutes I retreat
                    Unto that hour
Which shew'd thee last, but did defeat
                    Thy light, and pow'r,
I search, and rack my soul to see
                    Those beams again,
But nothing but the snuff to me
                    Appeareth plain;
That dark, and dead sleeps in its known,
                    And common urn,
But those fled to their Makers throne,
                    There shine, and burn;
O could I track them! but souls must
                    Track one the other,
And now the spirit, not the dust
                    Must be thy brother.
Yet I have one *Pearle* by whose light
                    All things I see,
And in the heart of Earth, and night
                    Find Heaven, and thee.

The Favour.

O THY bright looks! thy glance of love
Shown, & but shown me from above!
Rare looks! that can dispense such joy
As without wooing wins the coy.
And makes him mourn, and pine and dye
Like a starv'd Eaglet, for thine eye.
Some kinde herbs here, though low & far,
Watch for, and know their loving star.
O let no star compare with thee!
Nor any herb out-duty me!

So shall my nights and mornings be
Thy time to shine, and mine to see.

The Bird.

HITHER thou com'st: the busie wind all night
Blew through thy lodging, where thy own warm wing
Thy pillow was. Many a sullen storm
(For which course man seems much the fitter born,)
   Rain'd on thy bed
   And harmless head.

And now as fresh and chearful as the light
Thy little heart in early hymns doth sing
Unto that *Providence,* whose unseen arm
Curb'd them, and cloath'd thee well and warm.
   All things that be, praise him; and had
   Their lesson taught them, when first made.

So hills and valleys into singing break,
And though poor stones have neither speech nor tongue,
While active winds and streams both run and speak,
Yet stones are deep in admiration.
Thus Praise and Prayer here beneath the Sun
Make lesser mornings, when the great are done.

For each inclosed Spirit is a star
   Inlightning his own little sphære,
Whose light, though fetcht and borrowed from far,
   Both mornings makes, and evenings there.
But as these Birds of light make a land glad,
Chirping their solemn Matins on each tree:
So in the shades of night some dark fowls be,
Whose heavy notes make all that hear them, sad.

      The Turtle then in Palm-trees mourns,
         While Owls and Satyrs howl;

The pleasant Land to brimstone turns
And all her streams grow foul.

Brightness and mirth, and love and faith, all flye,
Till the Day-spring breaks forth again from high.

The World.

I SAW Eternity the other night
Like a great *Ring* of pure and endless light,
    All calm, as it was bright,
And round beneath it, Time in hours, days, years
        Driv'n by the spheres
Like a vast shadow mov'd, In which the world
        And all her train were hurl'd;
The doting Lover in his queintest strain
        Did their Complain,
Neer him, his Lute, his fancy, and his flights,
        Wits sour delights,
With gloves, and knots the silly snares of pleasure
        Yet his dear Treasure
All scatter'd lay, while he his eys did pour
        Upon a flowr.

2.

The darksome States-man hung with weights and woe
Like a thick midnight-fog mov'd there so slow
    He did not stay, nor go;
Condemning thoughts (like sad Ecclipses) scowl
        Upon his soul,
And Clouds of crying witnesses without
    Pursued him with one shout.
Yet dig'd the Mole, and lest his ways be found
        Workt under ground,
Where he did Clutch his prey, but one did see
        That policie,

Churches and altars fed him, Perjuries
>Were gnats and flies,
It rain'd about him bloud and tears, but he
>Drank them as free.

3.

The fearfull miser on a heap of rust
Sate pining all his life there, did scarce trust
>His own hands with the dust,
Yet would not place one peece above, but lives
>In feare of theeves.
Thousands there were as frantick as himself
>And hug'd each one his pelf,
The down-right Epicure plac'd heav'n in sense
>And scornd pretence
While others slipt into a wide Excesse
>Said little lesse;
The weaker sort slight, triviall wares Inslave
>Who think them brave,
And poor, despised truth sate Counting by
>Their victory.

4.

Yet some, who all this while did weep and sing,
And sing, and weep, soar'd up into the *Ring*,
>But most would use no wing.
O fools (said I,) thus to prefer dark night
>Before true light,
To live in grots, and caves, and hate the day
>Because it shews the way,
The way which from this dead and dark abode
>Leads up to God,
A way where you might tread the Sun, and be
>More bright than he.
But as I did their madnes so discusse
>One whisper'd thus,

This Ring the Bride-groome did for none provide
  But for his bride.

John Cap. 2. ver. 16, 17.
  All that is in the world, the lust of the flesh, the lust
of the Eys, and the pride of life, is not of the father,
but is of the world.
  And the world passeth away, and the lusts thereof,
but he that doth the will of God abideth for ever.

THE
Poetry
of
RICHARD CRASHAW

Wishes.

To his (supposed) Mistresse.

WHO ere shee bee,
That not impossible shee
That shall command my heart and mee;

Where ere shee lye,
Lock't up from mortall Eye,
In shady leaves of Destiny:

Till that ripe Birth
Of studied fate stand forth,
And teach her faire steps to our Earth;

Till that Divine
Idæa, take a shrine
Of Chrystall flesh, through which to shine:

Meet you her my wishes,
Bespeake her to my blisses,
And bee yee call'd my absent kisses.

I wish her Beauty,
That owes not all his Duty
To gaudy Tire, or glistring shoo-ty.

Something more than
Taffata or Tissew can,
Or rampant feather, or rich fan.

More than the spoyle
Of shop, or silkewormes Toyle
Or a bought blush, or a set smile.

A face thats best
By its owne beauty drest,
And can alone commend the rest.

A face made up
Out of no other shop,
Then what natures white hand sets ope.

A cheeke where Youth,
And Blood, with Pen of Truth
Write, what the Reader sweetly ru'th.

A Cheeke where growes
More then a Morning Rose:
Which to no Boxe his being owes.

Lipps, where all Day
A lovers kisse may play,
Yet carry nothing thence away.

Lookes that oppresse
Their richest Tires but dresse
And cloath their simplest Nakednesse.

Eyes, that displaces
The Neighbour Diamond, and out faces
That Sunshine by their owne sweet Graces.

Tresses, that weare
Iewells, but to declare
How much themselves more pretious are.

Whose native Ray,
Can tame the wanton Day
Of Gems, that in their bright shades play.

Each Ruby there,
Or Pearle that dare appeare,
Bee its owne blush, bee its owne Teare.

A well tam'd Heart,
For whose more noble smart,
Love may bee long chusing a Dart.

Eyes, that bestow
Full quivers on loves Bow;
Yet pay lesse Arrowes then they owe.

Smiles, that can warme
The blood, yet teach a charme,
That Chastity shall take no harme.

Blushes, that bin
The burnish of no sin,
Nor flames of ought too hot within.

Ioyes, that confesse,
Vertue their Mistresse,
And have no other head to dresse.

Feares, fond and flight,
As the coy Brides, when Night
First does the longing lover right.

Teares, quickly fled,
And vaine, as those are shed
For a dying Maydenhead.

Dayes, that need borrow,
No part of their good Morrow,
From a fore spent night of sorrow.

Dayes, that in spight
Of Darkenesse, by the Light
Of a cleere mind are Day all Night.

Nights, sweet as they,
Made short by lovers play,
Yet long by th'absence of the Day.

Life, that dares send
A challenge to his end,
And when it comes say *Welcome Friend*.

Sydnæan showers
Of sweet discourse, whose powers
Can Crowne old Winters head with flowers,

Soft silken Houres,
Open sunnes; shady Bowers,
Bove all; Nothing within that lowres.

What ere Delight
Can make Dayes forehead bright;
Or give Downe to the Wings of Night.

In her whole frame,
Have Nature all the Name,
Art and ornament the shame.

Her flattery,
Picture and Poesy,
Her counsell her owne vertue bee.

I wish, her store
Of worth, may leave her poore
Of wishes; and I wish —— No more.

Now if Time knowes
That her whose radiant Browes,
Weave them a Garland of my vowes;

Her whose just Bayes,
My future hopes can raise,
A trophie to her present praise;

Her that dares bee,
What these Lines wish to see:
I seeke no further, it is shee.

'Tis shee, and heere
Lo I uncloath and cleare,
My wishes cloudy Character.

May shee enjoy it,
Whose merit dare apply it,
But Modesty dares still deny it.

Such worth as this is,
Shall fixe my flying wishes,
And determine them to kisses.

Let her full Glory,
My fancyes, fly before yee,
Bee ye my fictions; But her story.

On Mr. G. Herberts booke intituled the Temple of Sacred Poems, sent to a Gentlewoman.

Know you faire, on what you looke;
Divinest love lyes in this booke:
Expecting fire from your eyes,
To kindle this his sacrifice.
When your hands unty these strings,
Thinke you have an Angell by th' wings.
One that gladly will bee nigh,
To wait upon each morning sigh.
To flutter in the balmy aire,
Of your well perfumed prayer.
These white plumes of his heele lend you,
Which every day to heaven will send you:
To take acquaintance of the spheare,
And all the smooth faced kindred there.
And though *Herberts* name doe owe
These devotions, fairest; know
That while I lay them on the shrine
Of your white hand, they are mine.

A Hymn to

THE NAME AND HONOR
of the admirable
SAINTE TERESA,
Foundresse *of the Reformation of the*
Discalced Carmelites,
both men & Women;

A WOMAN
for Angelicall heigth of speculation, for
Masculine courage of performance,
more then a woman.

who
Yet a child, out ran maturity, and
durst plott a Martyrdome;

The Hymne.

Loue, thou art Absolute sole lord
Of Life & Death. To proue the word,
Wee'l now appeal to none of all
Those thy old Souldiers, Great & tall,
Ripe Men of Martyrdom, that could reach down
With strong armes, their triumphant crown;
Such as could with lusty breath
Speak lowd into the face of death
Their Great Lord's glorious name, to none
Of those whose spatious Bosomes spread a throne
For Love at larg to fill: spare blood & sweat;
And see him take a priuate seat,
Making his mansion in the mild
And milky soul of a soft child.
   Scarse has she learn't to lisp the name

Of Martyr; yet she thinks it shame
Life should so long play with that breath
Which spent can buy so braue a death.
She neuer vndertook to know
What death with loue should haue to doe;
Nor has she e're yet vnderstood
Why to show loue, she should shed blood
Yet though she cannot tell you why,
She can Love, & she can Dy.

Scarse has she Blood enough to make
A guilty sword blush for her sake;
Yet has she'a Heart dares hope to proue
How much lesse strong is Death then Love.

Be loue but there; let poor six yeares
Be pos'd with the maturest Feares
Man trembles at, you straight shall find
Love knowes no nonage, nor the Mind.
'Tis Love, not Yeares *or* Limbs that can
Make the Martyr, or the man.

Love touch't her Heart, & lo it beates
High, & burnes with such braue heates;
Such thirsts to dy, as dares drink vp,
A thousand cold deaths in one cup.
Good reason. For she breathes All fire.
Her weake brest heaues with strong desire
Of what she may with fruitles wishes
Seek for amongst her Mother's kisses.

Since 'tis not to be had at home
She'l trauail to a Martyrdom.
No home for hers confesses she
But where she may a Martyr be.

She'el to the Moores; And trade with them,
For this vnualued Diadem.
She'l offer them her dearest Breath,
With Christ's Name in't, in change for death.
Shee'l bargain with them; & will giue
Them God; teach them how to liue
In him: or, if they this deny,

For him she'l teach them how to Dy.
So shall she leaue amongst them sown
Her Lord's Blood; or at lest her own.
    Farewel then, all the world! Adieu.
Teresa is no more for you.
Farewell, all pleasures, sports, & ioyes,
(Neuer till now esteemed toyes)
Farewell what euer deare may bee,
Mother's armes or Father's knee
Farewell house, & farewell home!
She's for the Moores, & Martyrdom.

    Sweet, not so fast! lo thy fair Spouse
Whom thou seekst with so swift vowes,
Calls thee back, & bidds thee come
T'embrace a milder Martyrdom.

    Blest powres forbid, Thy tender life
Should bleed vpon a barborous knife;
Or some base hand haue power to race
Thy Brest's chast cabinet, & vncase
A soul kept there so sweet, ô no;
Wise heaun will neuer haue it so
Thou art love's victime; & must dy
A death more mysticall & high.
Into loue's armes thou shalt let fall
A still-suruiuing funerall.
His is the Dart must make the Death
Whose stroke shall tast thy hallow'd breath;
A Dart thrice dip't in that rich flame
Which writes thy spouse's radiant Name
Vpon the roof of Heau'n; where ay
It shines, & with a soueraign ray
Beates bright vpon the burning faces
Of soules which in that name's sweet graces
Find euerlasting smiles. So rare,
So spirituall, pure, & fair
Must be th'immortall instrument
Vpon whose choice point shall be sent
A life so lou'd; And that there be

Fitt executioners for Thee,
The fair'st & first-born sons of fire
Blest SERAPHIM, shall leaue their quire
And turn loue's souldiers, vpon THEE
To exercise their archerie.
   O how oft shalt thou complain
Of a sweet & subtle PAIN.
Of intolerable IOYES;
Of a DEATH, in which who dyes
Loues his death, and dyes again.
And would for euer so be slain.
And liues, & dyes; and knowes not why
To liue, But that he thus may neuer leaue to DY.
   How kindly will thy gentle HEART
Kisse the sweetly-killing DART!
And close in his embraces keep
Those delicious Wounds, that weep
Balsom to heal themselues with. Thus
When These thy DEATHS, so numerous,
Shall all at last dy into one,
And melt thy Soul's sweet mansion;
Like a soft lump of incense, hasted
By too hott a fire, & wasted
Into perfuming clouds, so fast
Shalt thou exhale to Heaun at last
In a resoluing SIGH, and then
O what? Ask not the Tongues of men.
Angells cannot tell, suffice,
Thy selfe shall feel thine own full ioyes
And hold them fast for euer. There
So soon as thou shalt first appear,
The MOON of maiden starrs, thy white
MISTRESSE, attended by such bright
Soules as thy shining self, shall come
And in her first rankes make thee room;
Where 'mongst her snowy family
Immortall wellcomes wait for thee.
   O what delight, when reueal'd LIFE shall stand

And teach thy lipps heau'n with his hand;
On which thou now maist to thy wishes
Heap vp thy consecrated kisses.
What ioyes shall seize thy soul, when she
Bending her blessed eyes on thee
(Those second Smiles of Heau'n) shall dart
Her mild rayes through thy melting heart!

Angels, thy old friends, there shall greet thee
Glad at their own home now to meet thee.

All thy good WORKES which went before
And waited for thee, at the door,
Shall own thee there; and all in one
Weaue a constellation
Of CROWNS, with which the KING thy spouse
Shall build vp thy triumphant browes.

All thy old woes shall now smile on thee
And thy paines sitt bright vpon thee
All thy sorrows here shall shine,
All thy SVFFERINGS be diuine.
TEARES shall take comfort, & turn gemms
And WRONGS repent to Diademms.
Eu'n thy DEATHS shall liue; & new
Dresse the soul that erst they slew.
Thy wounds shall blush to such bright scarres
As keep account of the LAMB's warres.

Those rare WORKES where thou shalt leaue writt,
Loue's noble history, with witt
Taught thee by none but him, while here
They feed our soules, shall cloth THINE there.
Each heaunly word by whose hid flame
Our hard Hearts shall strike fire, the same
Shall flourish on thy browes. & be
Both fire to vs & flame to thee;
Whose light shall liue bright in thy FACE
By glory, in our hearts by grace.

Thou shalt look round about, & see
Thousands of crown'd Soules throng to be
Themselues thy crown. Sons of thy vowes

The virgin-births with which thy soueraign spouse
Made fruitfull thy fair soul, goe now
And with them all about thee bow
To Him, put on (hee'l say) put on
(My rosy loue) That thy rich zone
Sparkling with the sacred flames
Of thousand soules, whose happy names
Heau'n keeps vpon thy score. (Thy bright
Life brought them first to kisse the light
That kindled them to starrs.) and so
Thou with the LAMB, thy lord, shalt goe;
And whereso'ere he setts his white
Stepps, walk with HIM those wayes of light
Which who in death would liue to see,
Must learn in life to dy like thee.

The

FLAMING HEART

VPON THE BOOK AND
Picture of the seraphicall saint

TERESA,

(AS SHE IS VSVALLY EX-
pressed with a SERAPHIM
biside her.)

WELL meaning readers! you that come as freinds
And catch the pretious name this peice pretends;
Make not too much hast to' admire
That fair-cheek't fallacy of fire.
That is a SERAPHIM, they say
And this the great TERESIA.
Readers, be rul'd by me; & make
Here a well-plac't & wise mistake
You must transpose the picture quite,
And spell it wrong to read it right;
Read HIM for her, & her for him;
And call the SAINT the SERAPHIM.

Painter, what didst thou vnderstand
To put her dart into his hand!
See, euen the yeares & size of him
Showes this the mother SERAPHIM.
This is the mistresse flame; & duteous he
Her happy fire-works, here, comes down to see.
O most poor-spirited of men!
Had thy cold Pencil kist her PEN
Thou couldst not so vnkindly err
To show vs This faint shade for HER
Why man, this speakes pure mortall frame;
And mockes with female FROST loue's manly flame.
One would suspect thou meant'st to paint
Some weak, inferiour, woman saint.

But had thy pale-fac't purple took
Fire from the burning cheeks of that bright Booke
Thou wouldst on her haue heap't vp all
That could be found SERAPHICALL;
What e're this youth of fire weares fair,
Rosy fingers, radiant hair,
Glowing cheek, & glistering wings,
All those fair & flagrant things,
But before all, that fiery DART
Had fill'd the Hand of this great HEART.
Doe then as equall right requires,
Since His the blushes be, & her's the fires,
Resume & rectify thy rude design;
Vndresse thy Seraphim into MINE.
Redeem this iniury of thy art;
Giue HIM the vail, giue her the dart.

Giue Him the vail; that he may couer
The Red cheeks of a riuall'd louer.
Asham'd that our world, now, can show
Nests of new Seraphims here below.

Giue her the DART for it is she
(Fair youth) shootes both thy shaft & THEE
Say, all ye wise & well-peirc't hearts
That liue & dy amidst her darts,
What is't your tastfull spirits doe proue
In that rare life of Her, and loue?
Say & bear wittnes. Sends she not
A SERAPHIM at euery shott?
What magazins of immortall ARMES there shine!
Heaun's great artillery in each loue-spun line.
Giue then the dart to her who giues the flame;
Giue him the veil, who kindly takes the shame.

But if it be the frequent fate
Of worst faults to be fortunate;
If all 's præscription; & proud wrong
Hearkens not to an humble song;
For all the gallantry of him,
Giue me the suffring SERAPHIM.

His be the brauery of all those Bright things,
The glowing cheekes, the glistering wings;
The Rosy hand, the radiant Dart;
Leaue Her alone The Flaming Heart.
  Leaue her that; & thou shalt leaue her
Not one loose shaft but loue's whole quiuer.
For in loue's feild was neuer found
A nobler weapon then a Wovnd.
Loue's passiues are his actiu'st part.
The wounded is the wounding heart.
O Heart! the æquall poise of lou'es both parts
Bigge alike with wounds & darts.
Liue in these conquering leaues; liue all the same;
And walk through all tongues one triumphant Flame
Liue here, great Heart; & loue and dy & kill;
And bleed & wound; and yeild & conquer still.
Let this immortall life wherere it comes
Walk in a crowd of loues & Martyrdomes.
Let mystick Deaths wait on't; & wise soules be
The loue-slain wittnesses of this life of thee.
O sweet incendiary! shew here thy art,
Vpon this carcasse of a hard, cold, hart,
Let all thy scatter'd shafts of light, that play
Among the leaues of thy larg Books of day,
Combin'd against this Brest at once break in
And take away from me my self & sin,
This gratious Robbery shall thy bounty be;
And my best fortunes such fair spoiles of me.
O thou vndanted daughter of desires!
By all thy dowr of Lights & Fires;
By all the eagle in thee, all the doue;
By all thy liues & deaths of loue;
By thy larg draughts of intellectuall day,
And by thy thirsts of loue more large then they;
By all thy brim-fill'd Bowles of feirce desire
By thy last Morning's draught of liquid fire;
By the full kingdome of that finall kisse
That seiz'd thy parting Soul, & seal'd thee his;

By all the heau'ns thou hast in him
(Fair sister of the SERAPHIM!)
By all of HIM we haue in THEE;
Leaue nothing of my SELF in me.
Let me so read thy life, that I
Vnto all life of mine may dy.

BIBLIOGRAPHICAL NOTE

The best introduction to seventeenth-century metaphysical poetry is to be found in the essay introductory to

Metaphysical Lyrics and Poems of the Seventeenth Century. Selected and edited, with an Essay, by H. J. C. GRIERSON (Oxford, Clarendon Press, 1921);

and in two Essays by Mr. T. S. ELIOT:

The Metaphysical Poets and *Andrew Marvell,* first published in 1924 in *Homage to John Dryden* (Hogarth Press), and since reissued in *Collected Essays* (Faber and Faber, 1932).

The most useful material about the individual poets here discussed is contained in the following editions of their works:

The Poems of John Donne. Edited by H. J. C. GRIERSON. 2 vols. Clarendon Press, 1912.

The Works of George Herbert. Edited with a Commentary by F. E. HUTCHINSON. Clarendon Press, 1941.

The Works of Henry Vaughan. Edited by L. C. MARTIN. 2 vols. Clarendon Press, 1914.

Poems, English, Latin and Greek. Edited by L. C. MARTIN. 1 vol. Clarendon Press, 1927.

Professor Grierson's text of Donne's poems is almost exactly reproduced in

John Donne, Dean of St. Paul's, Complete Poetry and Selected Prose. Edited by JOHN HAYWARD (The Nonesuch Press, 1929). This volume also contains a representative selection of Donne's letters in prose and verse.

Index

TO THE FIRST LINES

Index

JOAN BENNETT is a Fellow of Girton College, Cambridge, and Lecturer in English at Cambridge University, England. She was born in 1896, a member of the distinguished Frankau family, and married Henry Stanley Bennett in 1920. Mrs. Bennett was educated at Wycombe Abbey, and Girton College, Cambridge. She has been Visiting Lecturer in the University of Chicago in 1952, 1955, and 1958. Mrs. Bennett's publications include *Four Metaphysical Poets* (1934), *Virginia Woolf: Her Art as a Novelist* (1945), and *George Eliot: Her Mind and Her Art* (1948).

THE TEXT of this book was set on the Linotype in *Fairfield,* a typeface designed by the distinguished American artist and engraver Rudolph Ruzicka. He has designed and illustrated many books and has created a considerable list of individual prints in a variety of techniques. The book was composed, printed, and bound by The Colonial Press Inc., Clinton, Massachusetts. Paper manufactured by S. D. Warren Company. Cover design by JOSEPH LOW.

Vintage Books